Phonics Without Worksheets

Blends, Digraphs, & More

Written by

Carol Mader

Editor:

Alaska Hults

Illustrator:

Kate Flanagan

Project Director:

Carolea Williams

Special thanks to:

Celeste Johnson for her creative contributions and encouragement
Jeanie Washam and her first grade class at Westminster Christian School
Annie Williams and her first grade class at Madison Elementary School

Table of Contents

Introduction

The *Phonics Without Worksheets* series invites you to make phonics fun for your students through cooperative learning, hands-on craft-making, interactive games, and activities with multisensory appeal. *Blends, Digraphs, & More* is a resource book for teachers or any adults who help students learn to read. Rather than using a paper-and-pencil format, it features easy and quick-to-prepare games, crafts, and activities to help students learn the sounds (phonemes) of letters and letter combinations, providing a systematic, logical, sequential, and fun way to teach phonics. These activities complement any existing reading program.

Research shows that when learning involves more than one of the five senses students more readily acquire and retain information. *Blends, Digraphs, & More* encourages students to

- **hear** letters and words spoken and read.
- **see** letters and words in a variety of visual forms.
- **touch** and create letter-related crafts.
- **smell** food prepared to reinforce letter sounds.
- **taste** food prepared during the activities.

The activities in this resource incorporate a variety of methods to help you meet the needs of students with different learning styles. Many activities can be expanded to involve parents and enable them to share in the thrill of seeing their children blossom into readers. Students can apply their new knowledge right away while reading the minibooks—short stories with a repetitive presentation of specific blends and digraphs—and completing the suggested picture-card activities. Use your favorite children's literature to further extend your students' experiences with language and letters. Look for this symbol to find tips for quickly modifying activities when you are working with one student.

The *Phonics Without Worksheets* series involves students in their own learning by engaging their senses and emotions to bring meaning to their interactions with the sounds and images of language.

How to Use This Book

Use the sequenced activities presented in *Blends, Digraphs, & More* to create an organized phonics program in which students are taught to associate letters with letter sounds. These sounds are also called phonemes. To teach the phoneme activities in *Blends, Digraphs, & More,* read each activity ahead of time; gather the necessary materials; and make any modifications your teaching space, time, or resources might require. As you read the activities, note that a letter or group of letters contained within two slashes refers to the sound a student hears—as in /a/ for the vowel sound in *sleigh* and /f/ for the beginning sound in *phone*.

Sight words are those words that do not obey phonetic rules. They must be memorized as a whole word to be recognized by sight. For example, if read phonetically, *done* would be pronounced as if it rhymed with *bone*. If a student tries to spell it phonetically, he or she would spell it *dun*. Pages 7 and 8 contain hands-on activities that can be used to teach the sight words listed on page 9.

Mini-books (pages 62–67) are small reproducible books that provide repeated use of specific letters or letter groups. They are provided as an added reinforcement, and the accompanying review activities give students additional practice in working with the letters they are learning to use. The mini-books can be colored and assembled by students. See page 61 for a variety of educational and enjoyable activities that incorporate the mini-books.

Picture cards (pages 71–80) with images of familiar objects whose names tend to be well-known by students are also included. Invite students to say aloud the name of the object on each picture card and listen for the sounds they hear in the name. Letter cards and activity ideas (pages 68–70) are provided for use with the picture cards to extend learning.

Here are some tips for incorporating this resource into your phonics program:

- *Anticipate*—Read each activity ahead of time to know what to expect. Encourage parents to donate any materials your class might need.
- *Brainstorm*—When introducing a new phoneme or blend, write the letter(s) on the board and tell students what sound it makes. Ask students to name words that include this phoneme. Write their suggestions on the board, and discuss words they suggest that do not have that phoneme—students learn from these attempts, too. If students get stuck, write the short and long vowels across the board. Add the phoneme or blend to each vowel, and challenge students to think of a word that starts with those sounds. When brainstorming words with vowel digraphs such as *oo*, write common consonants or consonant blends on the board, blend them with the vowel sound, and challenge students to think of a word that starts with that sound.
- *Read and Speak*—The sooner students can apply their knowledge of phonemes by seeing the letters in print and hearing them read by you, the better they'll retain the information. Invite students to locate specific letter sounds in stories, poems, and songs. Also, verbally emphasize the sound being taught in each lesson. For example, when you write and read *The Freight Train* (page 41), emphasize the long *a* sound. Wherever possible, emphasize the sound being taught through repetitive use in your directions to students. It adds fun to the activity and gives students further experience hearing the sound in context.
- *Assess*—Use the Student Progress Chart reproducible (page 6) to track the phonemes students have mastered. Keep the charts on a clipboard by your desk. Update the charts as students work on the activities. When a student misses a lesson, photocopy and send home the activity page as homework. This involves parents and invites them to play a part in teaching their child to read.

 Name ____________________

Student Progress Chart

Letters	Date Introduced	Date Reviewed	Date Mastered
Consonant Digraphs			
th			
ch			
sh			
wh			
ng			
ph			
Consonant Blends			
Vowel Digraphs			
aw/au			
ea (head)			
eigh			
ew/ui			
igh			
oi/oy			
oo (tooth)			
oo (book)			
ow (tow)			
ou/ow (cow)			
y			
Silent Letters			
t			
l			
b			
w			
k			
g			

Sight Word Activities

As your students progress, use the following activities to teach the sight words listed on page 9.

Sight Word Stickers

Distribute ten labels to each student. Write 15–20 sight words on the board. Read the sight words aloud with students. Invite students to choose ten words to write on their labels. Encourage students to decorate their labels. Then, distribute lined paper to each student. Ask students to write several sentences, using one to three sight words in each sentence, and place a label on the line where each sight word should go.

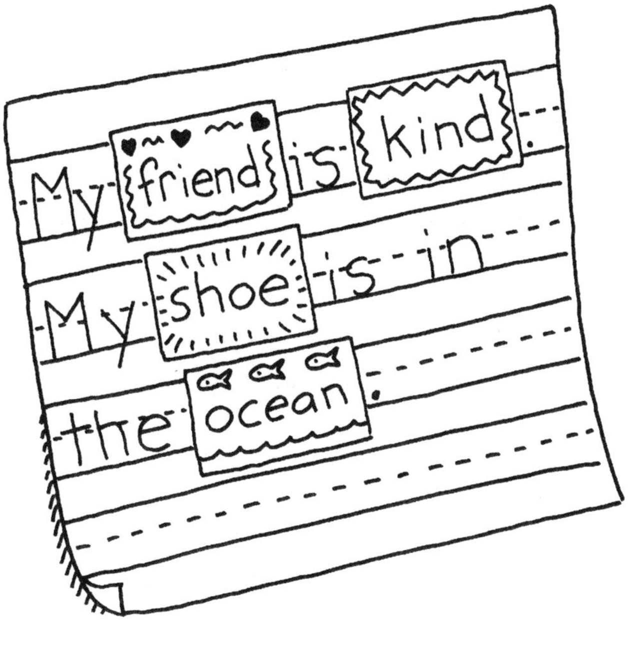

Readers Race the Runner

Write sight words on large index cards. Hold up each card, and read each word. Hand a card to each student. Ask one student to read aloud his or her card and then attach it to the chalkboard. Continue this until each card has been read and displayed. When students know most of the words, remove the cards and take the class to a large play area. The following activity is similar to "Duck-Duck-Goose." Have all students sit in a circle, and then have a volunteer stand up. Pass the cards around, one to each sitting student. At your signal have students begin to read their word one at a time, starting with the player to the left of the standing student. Have the volunteer run around the outside of the circle. Encourage the runner to reach the empty spot before the rest of the class finishes reading all the words. After each round, choose a new runner and pass cards one player to the right.

After reviewing the words with the student, challenge him or her to read aloud all the cards before you complete 15 jumping jacks (or a similar activity).

Look, a Book!

This activity helps students review consonant–vowel–consonant (CVC) words and sight words. Give each student three sheets of unlined paper. Have students fold their papers in half so that the dimensions are 8½" x 5½" (21.5 cm x 14 cm). Have students staple their papers together in the middle of the spine. Have students turn their book horizontally. Invite students to give their book their own title or write *Look, a Book!* Write on the board the sentences shown below and have students write one sentence on the bottom of each page. Have each student read his or her book to you.

- It was a sad day with no sun.
- We could not go see the ocean.
- Our kind mom took us to the store.
- We saw a boy with a box there.
- The box had many pretty cats.
- Now we have one new cat.

Word-Wall Chant and Boogie

Add several sight words to your word wall. Point to each word, and have students stamp, clap, and chant as they spell the word. To make the activity even more interactive, assign each letter one of the following categories of high (e.g., capital letters, *t, h, b,* and *d*), medium (e.g., *a, c, e,* and *i*), or low (e.g., *y, j,* and *g*). As students chant the letters for each word, have them bounce on their toes while standing straight for the high letters, bounce with bent hips and knees for medium letters, and crouch low to the ground for low letters.

Sight Words

any	find	mind	shoe	very
built	four	most	should	want
busy	friend	move	soup	was
child	from	none	sure	were
come	give	ocean	their	what
could	have	once	there	where
does	heart	pretty	they're	who
done	kind	put	to	why
door	love	said	too	wild
eyes	many	says	two	would

Thread the Word

th Consonant Digraph

Materials

- ✔ yarn
- ✔ scissors
- ✔ chart paper
- ✔ colored markers
- ✔ paper plates
- ✔ rulers
- ✔ brass fasteners

Preparation

Cut a length of yarn for each student about 2' (⅔ m) long. Draw on chart paper a very large happy face with a tongue sticking out.

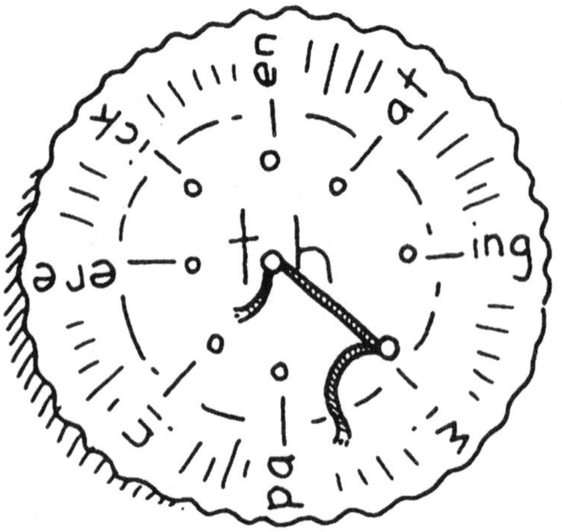

Display the chart paper, and write a *th* at the tip of the tongue. Ask volunteers to tell you the sounds the letters make separately. Then, tell students that together the letters make a new sound, /th/. Have the class practice the *th* sound and brainstorm words that begin or end with *th*. Write their suggestions on or around the happy face tongue. Use a different color to write *th* at the beginning of each word than *th* at the end. Give each student a paper plate, and show students how to use a ruler and light pencil lines to divide their plate into eight sections. Then, have students use a marker to write *th* in the middle of their plate. Ask students to choose eight *th* words and write them on the edges of their plate, replacing the *th* in each word with a line (see illustration). Give each student nine brass fasteners and a piece of yarn. Have students poke the brass fasteners through the plate at the end of each *th* line. Finally, have them poke a brass fastener through the center of the *th* and tie one end of the yarn to it. Invite students to complete each *th* word by twisting the free end of the yarn around the brass fastener by each word beginning or ending.

Th words include the following:

both	than	them	thick	this
cloth	thank	then	thin	those
math	that	there	thing	three
moth	the	these	think	thunder
path	their	they	third	with

The Thing

th Consonant Digraph

Give each student a paper plate, 10–15 toothpicks, and a ball of clay or dough. Have students write the title *The Toothpick Thing* across the upper edge of their plate. Ask students to divide their clay or dough in half, shape one half into a monster, arrange it on their plate, and stick toothpicks all over it. Have students form the letters *th* with the remaining clay or dough and place the letters on the lower edge of their plate. Then, guide the class in writing an interactive story about a monster. Encourage students to use *th* words, and record the story on chart paper. Have volunteers locate and highlight the *th*s in the monster story. Ask the class to count the total number of *th*s. Then, have each student write and illustrate his or her own list of *th* words. Keep each student's work in a "Blends and Digraphs Dictionary" folder. As students complete additional digraph and consonant blend activities, have them add to this folder. Instructions for the Blends and Digraphs Dictionary are on page 35.

Materials

- ✔ clay or dough (recipe below)
- ✔ paper plates
- ✔ toothpicks
- ✔ chart paper
- ✔ highlighter
- ✔ lined paper
- ✔ crayons or markers
- ✔ folders

Preparation

To prepare your own dough, mix 1 cup (250 ml) flour with ½ cup (125 ml) salt. Stir in 1 tablespoon (15 ml) oil. Measure ½ cup (125 ml) water, and add food coloring to the water if desired. Pour in the water and mix. This recipe yields dough for four students.

Ice-Cream Chart

ch Consonant Digraph

Materials

- ✔ Choosing Chart reproducible (page 13)
- ✔ chart paper
- ✔ lined paper
- ✔ crayons or markers
- ✔ folders
- ✔ chocolate or cherry ice cream, bowls, napkins, and spoons (optional)

Preparation

Photocopy the Choosing Chart reproducible for each student.

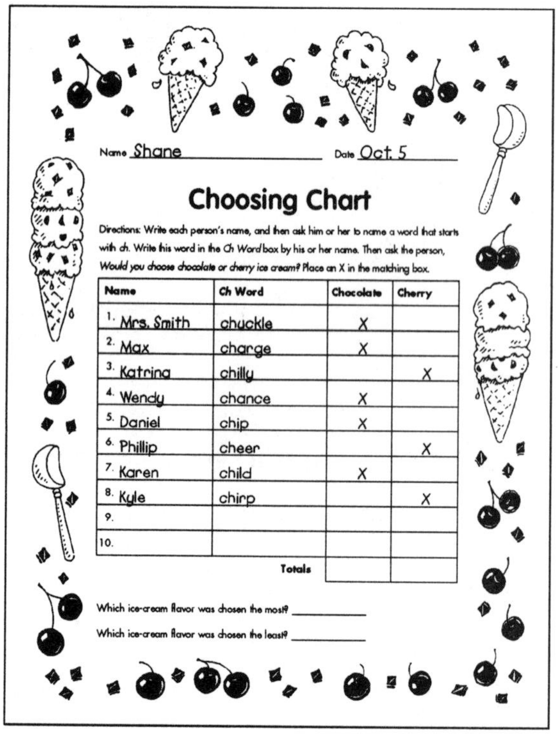

Name Shane Date Oct. 5

Choosing Chart

Directions: Write each person's name, and then ask him or her to name a word that starts with *ch*. Write this word in the *Ch Word* box by his or her name. Then ask the person, *Would you choose chocolate or cherry ice cream?* Place an X in the matching box.

Name	Ch Word	Chocolate	Cherry
1. Mrs. Smith	chuckle	X	
2. Max	charge	X	
3. Katrina	chilly		X
4. Wendy	chance	X	
5. Daniel	chip	X	
6. Phillip	cheer		X
7. Karen	child	X	
8. Kyle	chirp		X
9.			
10.			
	Totals		

Which ice-cream flavor was chosen the most? ________

Which ice-cream flavor was chosen the least? ________

Write *Choose Chocolate or Cherry* on the board, read it aloud, and invite volunteers to locate and circle the *ch*s. Give each student a Choosing Chart reproducible. Explain that students will be asking other people to choose between chocolate and cherry as a preferred ice-cream flavor. Invite students to predict which flavor will be more popular. Have the class interview you first. Tell students to write your name in the first column. Then, have students ask you to name a *ch* word. Students should write this word in the second column. Have students ask *Would you choose chocolate or cherry ice cream?* and then check the appropriate box when you give your answer. Check that students follow directions, and then have them interview their classmates, go to another classroom to interview students, or interview their families as homework. When the charts are complete, tally the results from all the charts to find the more popular ice cream. Then, have each student share his or her list of *ch* words, and add each new *ch* word to a class list on chart paper. Finally, have students write and illustrate their own list of *ch* words. Add their work to their Blends and Digraphs Dictionary folder. If you wish, serve the winning ice cream to everyone.

Name ______________________ Date ______________

Choosing Chart

Directions: Write each person's name, and then ask him or her to name a word that starts with *ch*. Write this word in the *Ch Word* box by his or her name. Then ask the person, *Would you choose chocolate or cherry ice cream?* Place an X in the matching box.

Name	***Ch* Word**	**Chocolate**	**Cherry**
1.			
2.			
3.			
4.			
5.			
6.			
7.			
8.			
9.			
10.			
	Totals		

Which ice-cream flavor was chosen the most? ______________

Which ice-cream flavor was chosen the least? ______________

Chunky Chocolate Chips

ch Consonant Digraph

Materials

- ✔ large bag of chocolate chips
- ✔ bowl
- ✔ chart paper
- ✔ highlighter

Preparation

none

Write *ch* on the board, and invite volunteers to tell you the sounds the letters make separately. Then, tell students that together the letters make a new sound, /ch/. Invite students to brainstorm *ch* words, and record their suggestions on the board. Toss students a chocolate chip each time they say a *ch* word. Have the class read aloud the *ch* words together. Pass around a bowl of chocolate chips. Invite each student to choose one to three chips and say a *ch* word for each chip. Then, guide the class in an interactive writing project about their favorite *ch* foods (e.g., cheese, chicken, cherries, and chocolate chips) and how they prepare them. Encourage students to use *ch* words in the story's text, and record the story on chart paper. Have volunteers highlight the *ch*s.

Shine the Shadows

sh Consonant Digraph

Write *sh* on the board, and invite volunteers to tell you the sounds the letters make separately. Then, tell students that together the letters make a new sound, /sh/. Invite students to brainstorm *sh* words, and record their suggestions on the board. Turn out the lights in the classroom, and pass one beginning or ending of a *sh* word to each student. Shuffle the transparency cards with complete *sh* words. Display one card on an overhead projector, and read it aloud. Have students look at their transparency card to see if it has part of that word. Have the student with the corresponding card come to the projector and place his or her card below your *sh* word card. Give the student the *sh* card to place in front of or at the end of his or her card to complete the word. Have the class read the word aloud. Repeat the process with the next word.

Sh words include the following:

dash	mash	she	shin
dish	rush	shed	ship
fish	shall	shelf	shop
hush	shark	shell	wish

Write each sh *word on a pair of index cards. Trim the* sh *from the second card of each pair. Keep one* sh *piece, and discard the rest. Shuffle the cards with the complete* sh *words, and invite the student to pick a card of his or her choice. Lay out the* sh *beginning and all the endings, and invite the student to find the right ending to complete each word. Repeat with a new word.*

Materials

- ✔ overhead transparencies and projector
- ✔ scissors

Preparation

Create a list of *sh* words. Create a pair of transparency cards for each *sh* word by cutting overhead transparencies into eight or ten equal pieces and writing one *sh* word on each piece. When every word has been written once, return to the beginning of the list and write each word on a second transparency card, but leave the *sh* off the word. Finally, make one transparency card that says *sh*.

Ssshh, a Shark!

sh Consonant Digraph

Materials

- ✔ Shark! reproducible (page 17)
- ✔ overhead transparency and projector
- ✔ yardstick or pointer
- ✔ paper
- ✔ crayons or markers
- ✔ lined paper
- ✔ folders

Preparation

Photocopy the Shark! reproducible to an overhead transparency.

Display the Shark! transparency, and read the story aloud. Invite volunteers to retell the story to you in their own words. Reread the first sentence aloud, and have volunteers show you the *sh*s in it by pointing to them on the overhead screen with a yardstick or pointer. Underline or circle the *sh*s they find. Then, distribute paper to students and turn off the overhead projector. Tell students that every time they hear /sh/, they are to write *sh* on their paper. Read the story aloud again, reading slowly and emphasizing the *sh* sound. After the story, have students count the *sh*s they have written. If they heard and recorded every *sh*, they will have 42. Then, have students write and illustrate their own list of *sh* words. Add their work to their Blends and Digraphs Dictionary folder.

Shark!

I was wading along the shore searching for shells in the shallow water. I splashed over to some wood that had been washed up on the shore. An old shipwreck! I shoved a piece of wood a short way into the waves. What was that shape shimmering in the shadows below? I froze. A shark! Its fin flashed, swishing in the sunshine. What should I do? Should I shout? Should I rush away? I shuddered to think of the sharp teeth. I shrieked and dashed to shore. The shark rushed after me! The shark's sharp teeth slashed at my shoes and shirt. I reached the shore and the shark swam away. I knew that sharks eat fish and shrimp. Now I know that sharks also like shoes and shirts.

Whirlybird

wh Consonant Digraph

Materials

- ✔ Whirlybird reproducible (page 19)
- ✔ scissors
- ✔ clear tape
- ✔ crayons or markers
- ✔ lined paper
- ✔ folders

Preparation

Photocopy the Whirlybird reproducible, and cut it into individual whirlybird patterns. Provide one pattern for each student.

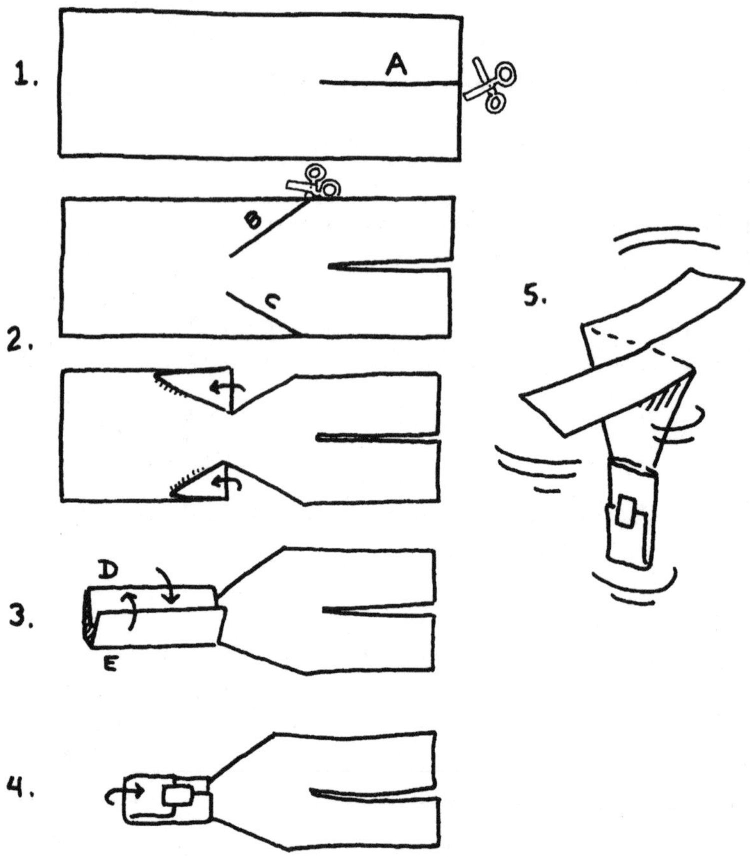

Have students brainstorm *wh* words, and write their suggestions on the board. Distribute the whirlybird patterns, and have students write *wh* words all over their whirlybird. Then, model each step for students before having them follow your directions.

1. Cut along line A.
2. Cut along lines B and C and fold down the triangles to the same side.
3. Fold the long sides in along lines D and E.
4. Fold the bottom up about 1" (2.5 cm) and secure with tape.
5. Fold the top blades down in opposite directions.

Invite students to gently toss their whirlybird into the air. Challenge students to name as many *wh* words as they can before their whirlybird lands. Then, have students write and illustrate their own list of *wh* words. Add their work to their Blends and Digraphs Dictionary folder.

Whirlybird

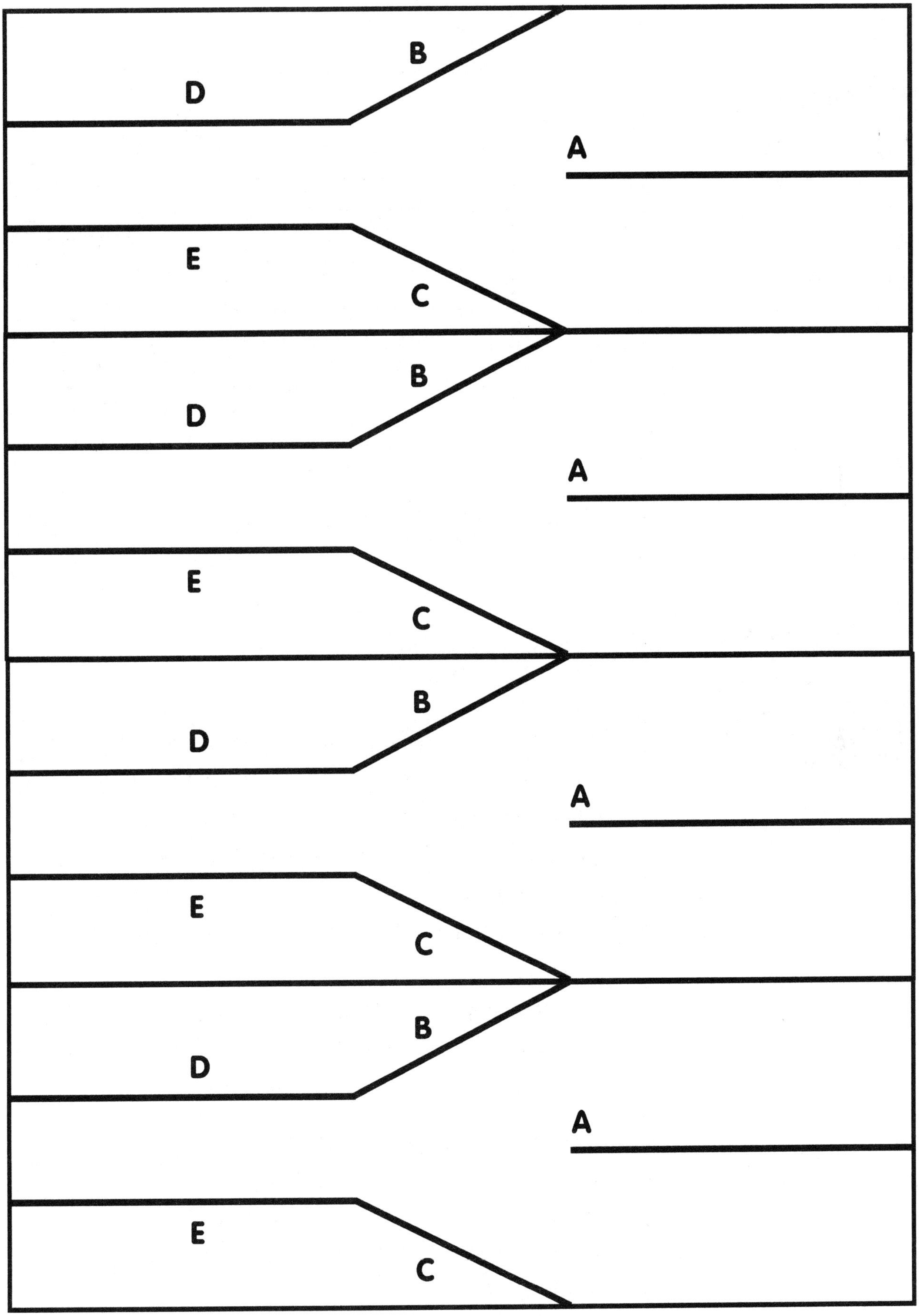

Where's the Whistler?

wh Consonant Digraph

Materials

- ✔ whistle (optional)
- ✔ die

Preparation

none

Write *wh* on the board, and invite volunteers to tell you the sounds the letters make separately. Then, tell students that together the letters make a new sound, /wh/. Invite students to brainstorm *wh* words, and record their suggestions on the board. Write *Where's the whistler?* on the board, and invite a volunteer to underline the *wh*s. Ask students to close their eyes. Silently choose a student to become the whistler. Ask him or her to whistle two times. (You might want to provide a whistle for students who aren't proficient whistlers.) Students then open their eyes and guess who was the whistler. If they are not able to, ask the whistler to reveal himself or herself. Give the whistler a die, and invite him or her to roll it and read that number of *wh* words to the class. After they have closed their eyes again, the whistler gives the die to another student who becomes the next whistler. Play until everyone has had a chance to be the whistler.

Wh words include the following:

whale	wheel	which	whirl	white
what	when	while	whisker	whopper
wheat	where	whip	whisper	why

Have the student hide and then blow a whistle once. Go looking for your whistler! After the student reads the wh words, switch places.

Clang and Bang

ng Consonant Digraph

Materials

- ✔ chart paper
- ✔ scissors
- ✔ noisemaker (e.g., big pot lid)
- ✔ 2 wooden spoons
- ✔ lined paper
- ✔ crayons or markers
- ✔ folders

Preparation

Cut a piece of chart paper vertically down the middle.

Have students brainstorm *ang* and *ung* words, and record their suggestions on the board. Divide the class into two teams, the Clangers and the Bangers. Distribute a strip of chart paper to each team, and have the teams write the brainstormed words in a column on their paper. Both teams should have identical lists. Post the lists on one side of the room and a noisemaker on the other side. Have a volunteer model the following steps: read all the words on the list, run with a wooden spoon to the noisemaker, bang it, run back to the group, and hand the spoon to the next student who will repeat these steps. Have the teams line up next to their word list, and start the race. Give all students a turn, even after one team has finished. Then, have students write and illustrate their own list of *ng* words. Add their work to their Blends and Digraphs Dictionary folder.

Ang/ung words include the following:

bang	hang	pang	sang
clang	hanger	rang	strung
clung	lung	rung	sung

Play this game the same way but divide the list of words into three columns. Use a stopwatch to time the student, and challenge him or her to complete each successive run faster, reading one column on each run.

King Kong

ng Consonant Digraph

Materials

- ✔ King Kong reproducible (page 23)
- ✔ scissors
- ✔ plastic stacking blocks
- ✔ wipe-off crayons
- ✔ paper towels

Preparation

Photocopy the King Kong reproducible, and cut out one pattern for each student. Assemble a collection of plastic stacking blocks.

Write *ng* on the board, and invite volunteers to tell you the sounds the letters make separately. Then, tell students that together the letters make a new sound, /ng/. Invite students to brainstorm *ing* and *ong* words, and record their suggestions on the board. Briefly tell students about a silly monkey named King Kong who liked to leave the zoo and swing from building to building in the city. Tell students they will build *ing/ong* towers for King Kong to climb. Give each student several plastic stacking blocks and a wipe-off crayon. Invite students to write *ing* and *ong* words on their blocks and then use them to build a tower. Give each student a King Kong pattern, and invite students to make him climb their tower while they read the words. Have students wipe off their words with a paper towel.

Ing/ong words include the following:

along	ding	ring	string	wing
belong	fling	sing	strong	wrong
bring	long	song	swing	
cling	ping	sting	thing	

King Kong

Phony *F*

ph Consonant Digraph

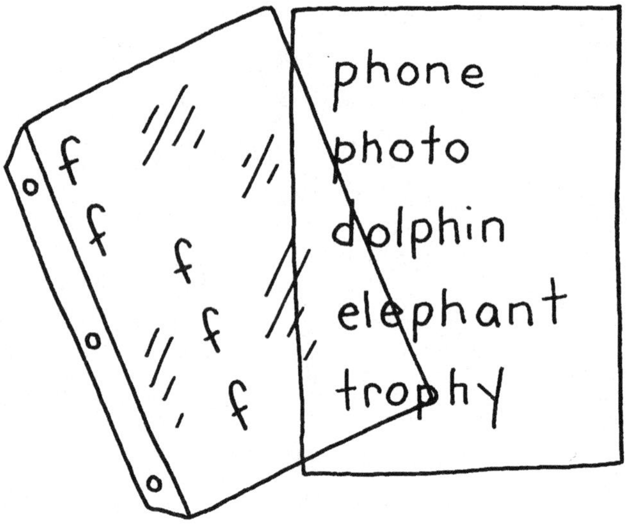

Materials

- ✔ markers
- ✔ paper
- ✔ transparent page protectors
- ✔ wipe-off crayons
- ✔ paper towels

Preparation

none

Write *ph* on the board, and invite volunteers to tell you the sounds the letters make separately. Then, tell students that together the letters make the sound /f/. Have students brainstorm *ph* words, and offer hints and clues where necessary. Encourage students to think of words that may not begin with *ph* but have *ph* in them. Then, ask them to use markers to copy the words onto a piece of paper. When finished, give each student a page protector and wipe-off crayon. Have students slide their paper into the page protector. On top of the page protector, have students use their crayon to write an *f* everywhere they see a *ph*. Encourage students to read all the words to a neighbor and then use a paper towel to erase the *f*s on top of the "phony" *f* words.

Ph words include the following:

alphabet	gopher	orphan	photograph
dolphin	Joseph	phone	phrase
elephant	nephew	phony	trophy

Photographs and Autographs

ph Consonant Digraph

Write *Photographs and Autographs of My Friends* on the board. Give each student a class photograph book, and have students copy the title for their book. Have students decorate the cover and circulate around the room, asking for autographs, phone numbers, and notes from their friends. Have students write *my photograph* and their name on the back of their picture and tape it to the bulletin board. Have students sign their name near their picture. Then, have students write and illustrate their own list of *ph* words. Add their work to their Blends and Digraphs Dictionary folder.

Have the student make a Photographs and Autographs *book. Invite him or her to collect pictures and autographs of family and friends. The student can add phone numbers to the book.*

Materials

- ✔ student photographs
- ✔ colored construction paper
- ✔ stapler
- ✔ crayons or markers
- ✔ clear tape
- ✔ lined paper
- ✔ folders

Preparation

Ask parents to send in one photograph of their child. Tell parents that students will be writing on the back of their photograph. When all the photographs are collected, arrange two or three photographs on a piece of paper and photocopy them, making a copy for each student in the class. Continue until all the photographs have been photocopied, and collate the copies to make a complete set of photocopies for each student. Make a class photograph book for each student by stapling each set of photographs between two sheets of colored construction paper that are slightly larger than the photocopied paper. Prepare a bulletin board with the title *Our Photographs and Autographs.*

Foot Work

Consonant Blends

Materials

✔ index cards

Preparation

Write on separate index cards consonant blends, such as *bl, br, cr, cl,* and *tr*. Write on other index cards word endings, such as *-ick, -own, -ack,* and *-oon*. Laminate the cards for durability. Create a list of words that can be formed by putting these blends and endings together. (See page 35 for ideas.)

Write your word list on the board, and read it aloud to the class. Invite the class to reread it aloud to you. Discuss words with which students are unfamiliar. Then lay the blend cards on one table and word-ending cards on an adjacent table. Have each student take one index card from each table to form a word. Invite students to refer to the board for ideas. Some students may form nonsense words. Stand at the other end of the room. Have students stand in a line and put their blend under their left foot and their ending under their right foot. Have them shuffle across the room to you, keeping the cards under their feet and blending their word aloud. (It is not necessary for students to wait for the student ahead of them to get all the way to you.) When students get to the other side, have them tell you the word they've blended. (Students with nonsense words should pronounce them correctly.) To extend the learning, repeat the activity the next day and have students write their own blends and endings. Have them tear paper into palm-sized squares, write the blend on one square, and write the rest of the word on another square. Use the same list as the previous day, or invite students to generate their own words.

Lift the Flap

Consonant Blends

Spell out a word by taping an index card under each tagboard square. Lift the first flap, and invite students to guess what the word is. Allow students three or four guesses per flap before you lift the next flap and invite students to blend the letters and guess again. Repeat the activity with new words. Once students are familiar with the activity, turn it into a game by dividing the class into two teams and having one student at a time take a turn at guessing. Give each student three guesses per flap, and award a point to the team with the student who correctly guesses the word. Alternate play between teams on each flap so everyone has a chance to play.

Tally the amount of guesses it took the student to get each word right. Agree in advance on a privilege or other treat the student can earn if he or she guesses a word in three tries or less.

Materials

- ✔ index cards
- ✔ masking or correction tape
- ✔ four tagboard squares cut slightly larger than the index cards
- ✔ large cardboard rectangle
- ✔ envelope

Preparation

Write on separate index cards blends, such as *bl, cr, cl, tr,* and *tw* and each letter of the alphabet. Tape the top edge of four tagboard squares side by side on a large cardboard rectangle. The tagboard squares will serve as flaps to cover the index cards. Place all the index cards in an envelope, and attach it to the cardboard back. Then, make a list of five-letter words that begin with common blends. (See page 35 for ideas.)

Hand to Hand

Consonant Blends

Materials

✔ blank labels

Preparation

Divide blank labels into two sets so that each set contains one label for each student. Create a list of words that begin with consonant blends, such as *bl, br, cr, cl,* and *tr.* (See page 35 for ideas.) Write each beginning blend from the word list on the first set of labels and each corresponding ending on the second set. Shuffle each set separately.

Write your word list on the board, and have the class read it aloud. Discuss words with which students are unfamiliar. Erase the words on the board. Then, have students close their eyes and extend their hands, palms down. Place a blend label on each student's left hand and an ending label on each student's right hand. Be sure that the blend and ending do not form a real word. When all hands are labeled, have students open their eyes. Tell students that at your signal they will wander around the room, say their sounds, and look for a student with a label that forms a complete word when paired with one of their own labels. When two students form a word, have them give a "high five," say *good-bye* to that partner, and look for another student with whom to form a word. Tell students to listen for your signal to end the game. At your signal, have students find a mate, hold their partner's hands, and sit down.

Cut pairs of mittens out of construction paper. Have the student write the beginning blends on the left-handed mittens and the endings on the right-handed mittens. Hide them around the room, and challenge the student to find them and make complete words.

Sweet Blends

Consonant Blends

Materials

- ✔ cups
- ✔ alphabet cereal
- ✔ frosting
- ✔ paper plates
- ✔ plastic knives

Preparation

Fill a cup with alphabet cereal for each child. Fill a cup with frosting for each group of four or five students.

Divide the class into groups of four or five. Give each student a cup of cereal, a paper plate, and a plastic knife. Give each group a cup of frosting. Have students sort their letters to see how many of each letter they have while you write common blends on the board. Have students spread their frosting onto their plate. Invite students to place the cereal in the frosting to form blends and then use other letters to form complete words. Encourage students to write their words on the board for other students to spell. When students have five or more words spelled correctly on their plate, invite them to eat their words.

Sing-Song Write-Along

Consonant Blends

Materials

- ✔ chart paper
- ✔ lined paper

Preparation

Choose a familiar nursery rhyme or song that includes a variety of consonant blends, such as *One, Two, Buckle My Shoe; Twinkle, Twinkle Little Star;* or *Sleep, Baby, Sleep.* Write the words to the chant or song on chart paper.

Post the chart paper, and have volunteers locate and circle the consonant blends. Then, give each student a piece of lined paper. As you slowly sing the song, invite students to write down any blends they hear.

Locate an old copy of a book of nursery rhymes. Cut the pages out of the book, and place each in a clear page protector. Have the student read aloud each nursery rhyme with you. Then, ask him or her to locate the consonant blends and use a marker to underline them. Clean the page protectors with a paper towel, and store them in a binder for later use.

Illustration Creation

Consonant Blends

Label each section with a blend. Give each student a magazine, catalog, or printed advertisement. Ask students to locate pictures of objects whose names begin or end with one of the blends. Have students cut out the pictures, glue them to the corresponding section of the butcher paper, and label each picture. When the activity is complete, point to several of the pictures in each section and have the class read aloud each name.

Materials

- ✔ butcher paper
- ✔ markers
- ✔ magazines, catalogs, or printed advertisements
- ✔ scissors
- ✔ glue

Preparation

Write *Blend Friend* at the top of a large piece of butcher paper, and use a marker to divide the butcher paper into five to ten sections. Display the paper on the wall.

Criss Cross

Consonant Blends

Materials

✔ paper

Preparation

none

Write a consonant blend on the board. Have each student write five words that begin with that blend. When students are finished, call out words that begin with that blend. If a student has the word on his or her list, have him or her cross it out. After listing ten words, have students who have one or more words left stand, then two or more (students who have less than two will now sit), then three or more (students with two words sit), and so on until the students with the most words are left standing. Check the lists to be sure that all of the words are real words. Have these students select a new consonant blend for the next round.

Write blend words, cover the paper, and invite the student to do the same. Then, invite the student to compare the lists and cross off the words you have in common. Invite the student to select a new blend, and challenge him or her to think of words that begin with that blend.

Three Card Draw

Consonant Blends

Materials

- ✔ index cards
- ✔ clear or magnetic tape

Preparation

Write words with the same or similar endings on index cards. Make several sets. Use the word list at left or one of your own.

Use clear or magnetic tape to attach one set of three cards to the chalkboard. Say a sentence that uses only one of the words on the board. Have a volunteer identify which word was used in the sentence. After the student identifies the correct word, invite additional volunteers to correctly use the remaining words in new sentences. Consider a small prize for each word used correctly. Repeat with a new set of words.

Three card sets include:

blam	blast	last
clock	cloth	lock
crash	spill	splash
scream	screen	team
swan	swim	win
rain	trade	train

Concentration Education

Consonant Blends

Materials

✔ white and colored index cards

Preparation

Make pairs of cards by writing the onset of a word on a colored card and the rime on a white card. Keep a list of the words you use. Make a set of at least ten pairs for every four or five students in the class. Sort the cards into colored and white piles. (Be careful that the ink does not bleed through to the other side of the card.)

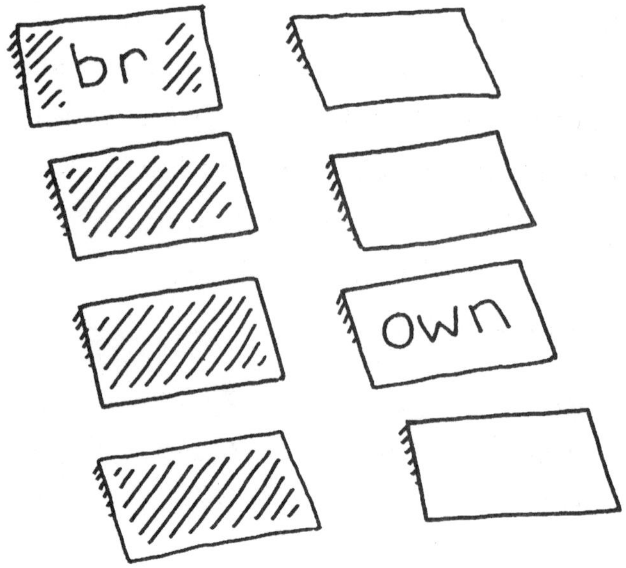

Divide the class into groups of four or five students, and distribute a set of cards to each group. Have students line the cards in rows facedown, colored cards on the left and white on the right. Ask students to take turns flipping over one card in each column to try and find a match that makes a real word. If no match is found, have the student return the card to the same spot. If a match is made, have the student keep the pair. Tell students that a player who makes a match gets another turn. Have students play until all cards are matched.

Blends Word List

Common blends include *bl, br, cl, cr, dr, fl, fr, gr, pr, sk, sl, sn, sp, st, str,* and *tr*. Common word endings include *-ack, -am, -ap, -ape, -at, -ee, -en, -ess, -ick, -ill, -im, -ine, -oon, -ot, -own,* and *-un*. Use these blends and endings to form words. Begin with words students already know. When you introduce a new word to students, discuss its meaning. Then, have each student create a list of words for each blend you choose. Invite students to illustrate some of their words. Add their words and illustrations to their Blends and Digraphs Dictionary folder. When you are ready to bind the finished dictionaries, have each student make a cover for his or her dictionary, and then bind each book individually for students to take home and read. Common blend families include the following:

bl	cl	dr	fr	pr	sl	sp	str
black	clang	dream	frame	press	sleep	speed	strap
blend	clap	dress	free	pretty	sleigh	spin	straw
blind	clean	drill	frog	price	slice	spoon	streak
blink	clear	drink	frost	pride	slide	sport	stream
bloom	clock	drop	frown	prince	slim	spot	street
blue	close	dry	fry	prize	sly	spy	string

br	cr	fl	gr	sk	sn	st	tr
brain	crab	flag	grade	skate	snack	stair	train
brave	crane	flat	grain	skill	snail	star	trap
bride	cream	flea	grape	skin	snake	start	trash
broke	creek	flip	gravy	skip	sneak	stir	tree
broom	crib	flute	green	skirt	snore	stone	tribe
brush	crown	fly	grill	sky	snug	stop	try

Launch the Thaumatrope

aw/au Vowel Digraphs

Materials

- ✔ Thaumatrope reproducible (page 37)
- ✔ cardstock
- ✔ scissors
- ✔ heavyweight string
- ✔ glue
- ✔ hole punch

Preparation

Photocopy the Thaumatrope reproducible onto cardstock. Each student will need two copies for a total of four circles. Cut string into four 10" (25.5 cm) lengths for each student.

Write on the board three to five *aw* and *au* words, such as *author, autumn, straw,* and *yawn.* Read them to students, and ask what vowel sound these words have in common. Underline the *aw* and *au* in the words. Then, have students brainstorm additional *aw* or *au* words, and add their suggestions to the list. Tell students they will be making a thaumatrope. Give each student two Thaumatrope reproducibles, glue, and four pieces of string. Ask students to choose one *aw* or *au* word. Have students write the *aw* or *au* of the word on the line in the center of circle B. Then, have students write the rest of the word on the line in the center of circle A. Remind students to omit the *aw* or *au* on circle A. Invite students to decorate the border of circle B. Have students cut out both circles and punch a hole in the small circles at the left and right side of each large circle. Have students place their circles back-to-back, place one circle upside down and one upright, align the two sets of holes, glue them together, and tie a string to each set of holes. Finally, have students hold both ends and twist the circle around until the strings are wound tight. Then, have students pull the strings outward. As they do, the circle will spin and students will see the *aw* or *au* word blend. Have students read aloud the word they see. Invite students to use the list on the board to choose a second *aw* or *au* word and make a second thaumatrope.

Thaumatrope

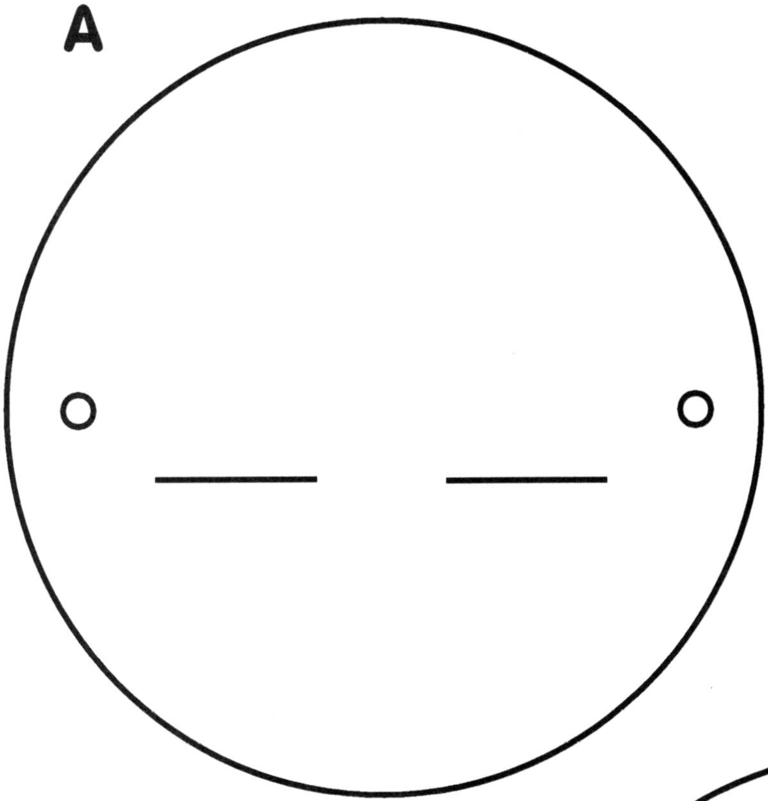

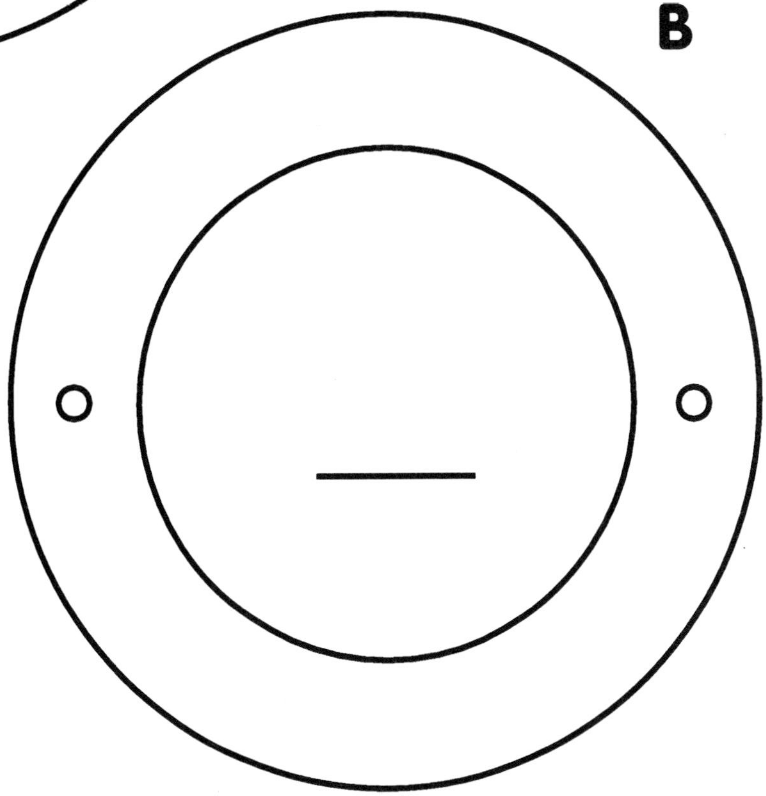

Ready for Treasure

Short *ea* Vowel Digraph

Materials

- ✔ Ready for Treasure reproducible (page 39)
- ✔ chart paper
- ✔ spools of thread
- ✔ healthy food items (e.g., carrots, raisins, cheese)
- ✔ individually wrapped mints
- ✔ chocolate coin "treasure"
- ✔ measurement tools (e.g., rulers, measuring tape, yardsticks, measuring cups, scales)

Preparation

Photocopy a class set of the Ready for Treasure reproducible. Write short *ea* words on chart paper (see word list at right for suggestions). Place spools of thread, healthy food items, mints, chocolate coins, and measurement tools on a table near the chart paper.

Display the short *ea* words, and read them aloud to students. Use the materials from the table to discuss with students the meanings of some of the words. Then, have students refer to the chart paper and tell you what sound the words have in common. Invite volunteers to underline the *ea* in each word. During a break, hide the items around the classroom. When students return, give each student a Ready for Treasure reproducible. Read aloud each line on the reproducible, and discuss how students can complete it by using previous knowledge, following the directions, or looking around the room for hidden items. Tell students to leave the items they find where they are for other students to locate. After all students have found the items, invite volunteers to tell their answers to the class. End the activity by sharing the chocolate coins or mints with students.

Short *ea* words include the following:

bread	feather	measure	sweater
breath	head	read	thread
dead	health	ready	treasure
deaf	heavy	steady	weather

Name ______________________ Date ______________

Ready for Treasure

1. Where did you find hidden thread?
2. Name a healthy food hidden in the classroom.
3. Name your favorite kind of bread.
4. Name something heavy you can find in the room.
5. Where did you find a tool that measures?
6. Write where you found a chocolate treasure.
7. Who is wearing a sweater?
8. Describe the weather.
9. Name a book you have read.

10. Find something as light as a feather. Write the name of what you found.
11. If something is not alive, it is ______________.
12. People who cannot hear are ______________.
13. Find something that cures bad breath and tell what you found.
14. Circle all the words on this page that have the *ea* sound as in *head*. How many did you find? Write the number here. ________

Neighborhood

eigh Vowel Digraph

Materials

- ✔ butcher paper
- ✔ construction paper
- ✔ scissors
- ✔ glue
- ✔ crayons or markers

Preparation

Write *Our Neighborhood* at the top of a large piece of butcher paper.

Draw simple homes on the board, and fill them in with *eigh* words, such as *neighbor, sleigh,* and *freight.* Tell students *eigh* makes the long *a* sound. Invite volunteers to locate and underline *eigh* in each of the words. Write *neighborhood* on the board, and read it aloud. Discuss with students what they feel makes up a neighborhood. Invite students to tell what buildings and people they would put in their neighborhood. Tell students they will make their own classroom neighborhood mural. Give students construction paper, and invite each student to use the paper, scissors, glue, and crayons or markers to make a house, business, or public building for the mural. Have them glue their completed building onto the butcher paper. Invite students who finish early to make street signs with *eigh* words (e.g., *Eighth* Avenue and *Freight* Station) and vehicles for the neighborhood scene.

The Freight Train

Long *a* Review

Give each student a copy of the Long *A* Review reproducible. Read it aloud, and then have the class reread it. When students have reviewed all the words, have them cut apart the cards and sort them by vowel pattern into four columns on their desk. Ask each student to show you his or her sorted columns. Then, invite students to add their cards to the correct freight car. To extend the learning, have students locate long *a* words in newspapers and other printed materials. Invite them to copy the words onto index cards and add them to the train.

Materials

- ✔ Long *A* Review reproducible (page 42)
- ✔ butcher paper
- ✔ 5 disposable loaf pans
- ✔ stapler
- ✔ construction paper
- ✔ scissors
- ✔ tape
- ✔ sentence strips
- ✔ glue
- ✔ cardboard tube
- ✔ cotton
- ✔ small milk carton (optional)

Preparation

Photocopy a class set of the Long *A* Review reproducible. Cover a wall with butcher paper. Create a freight train by turning a disposable loaf pan upside down and stapling one side of it to the wall. Staple four more loaf pans next to it, right side up. Cut out construction-paper wheels, and tape them to the sides of the pans. Draw a track on the butcher paper. Write *Our Freight Train* on a sentence strip, and tape it to the top of the display. Write *eigh, ay, ai,* and *a with silent e* on another sentence strip, cut it into individual cards, and tape a card to each car. Glue a cardboard tube with cotton trailing out of it on the front of the first loaf pan for a smokestack. To make the cab of the engine, cut the lid off of a small milk carton, cover it with construction paper, and glue it behind the smokestack.

Long *A* Review

ape	bake	eight	flake
freight	gain	main	neighbor
pail	pay	play	sail
shake	sleigh	spray	take
train	tray	way	weight

Chew Fruit

ew/ui Vowel Digraphs

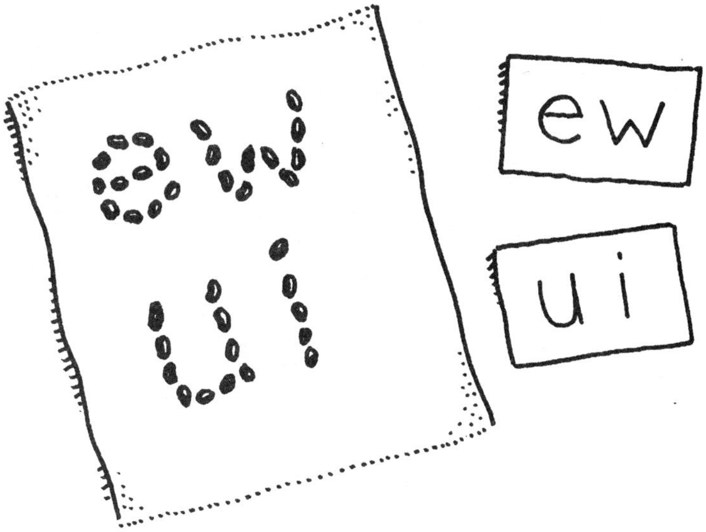

Display the *ew* and *ui* words in a pocket chart. Read the words aloud with students. Discuss words with which students may be unfamiliar. Tell students *ew* and *ui* make the /oo/ sound as in *toot*. Have students say /oo/. Review the *ew* words, pointing out the *ew* in each word, and then do the same for the *ui* words. Take the *chew* and *fruit* cards from the pocket chart, and use clear tape to attach them to the board. Tell students they will be chewing fruit to help them remember the sound the letters make. Give each student a cup of raisins, two blank index cards, and a paper towel. Read students one of the cards from the pocket chart, and have them form *ew* and *ui* with raisins on their paper towel. Have students write *ew* and *ui* on separate index cards. Remove all the cards from the pocket chart, shuffle them, display one at a time, and read aloud each word. Have students hold up either the *ew* or *ui* card to indicate which vowel pair is in the word. Invite students to chew on their fruit as they work. Consider ending the lesson with cups of juice.

Materials

- ✔ index cards
- ✔ colored markers
- ✔ raisins
- ✔ small paper cups
- ✔ pocket chart
- ✔ clear tape
- ✔ paper towels
- ✔ juice and cups (optional)

Preparation

Write *ew* words, such as *blew, chew, crew, drew, few, flew,* and *knew,* on separate index cards. Write the *ew* in a different color from the rest of the word. Do the same for *ui* words, such as *bruise, cruise, fruit, juice, juicy, pursuit,* and *suit,* writing the *ui* in a different color. Place a handful of raisins in a small paper cup for each student.

My High Kite

igh Vowel Digraph

Materials

- ✔ chart or butcher paper
- ✔ index cards
- ✔ adhesive putty or tape

Preparation

Write the story *My High Kite* on chart or butcher paper, leaving a blank spot the size of an index card at each bold word.

My High Kite

It was a windy day. The sun was **bright.** My dad and I decided to fly our kite. We ran with all our **might.** The kite was **light.** We did it **right.** The wind blew hard. The kite took **flight.** What a **delight!** We gave a **sigh,** and held on **tight.** The kite flew **high** and **higher.** We flew the kite all afternoon. Soon it would be **night.** There would be no **sunlight** and the kite would be out of **sight.** So we pulled the kite back to the ground, wrapping the string round and round.

Draw on the board a picture of a large eye. Write in the center the words in bold shown above. Tell students *igh* makes the long *i* sound and sounds like *eye.* (Write *eye* next to the picture so students do not confuse the spellings.) Invite volunteers to locate and underline *igh* in each of the words. Give each volunteer an index card on which to draw the outline of an eye. Assign each volunteer an *igh* word from the board to write on his or her index card. Display the story. Ask students to read silently as you read it aloud. Stop at each blank, and invite the class to decide which *igh* word best fills that blank. Have a volunteer use adhesive putty or tape to stick the correct card in the blank. Allow students to place an incorrect card in a blank. Students can move the cards later when they discover that the word is more appropriate in another sentence. When the blanks are filled in, read the story together.

Royal Soil

oi/oy Vowel Digraphs

Materials

- ✔ construction paper (assorted colors)
- ✔ scissors
- ✔ blue and brown butcher paper
- ✔ glue
- ✔ chart paper
- ✔ stapler

Preparation

Cut a 7½" x 18" (19 cm x 46 cm) yellow construction-paper strip for each student. Post a large piece of blue butcher paper on the wall, and glue a strip of brown butcher paper to the bottom to represent soil. Write across the top *Our Royal Soil,* and add a few decorations, such as a construction-paper fence or sun. Write 15–20 *oy* and *oi* words on chart paper.

Display the chart paper, and read aloud the *oy* and *oi* words. Tell students *oi* and *oy* make the same sound, and have them practice saying the sound. Then, tell students they will be planting a royal garden with *oi* and *oy* words. Give each student a strip. Invite students to copy ten words onto their paper and trim one edge of the paper to look like the points of a crown. Staple the ends of each student's paper into a tube shape, fitting each "crown" to the student's head. Distribute additional construction paper, and have students make colorful "flowers" with additional *oi* and *oy* words written on the stems. Stand by the Royal Soil mural, and invite students to read you the words they wrote on their crown or flower. After they have successfully read you their words, have them glue or staple their flowers to the brown "garden soil" of the mural.

Oy/oi words include the following:

annoy	coil	joint	oil	soil
boil	enjoy	joy	point	spoil
boy	foil	moist	rejoice	toilet
broil	join	noise	royal	toy

Balloon Boom

oo Vowel Digraph

Materials

- ✔ markers
- ✔ balloons
- ✔ pipe cleaners
- ✔ vase (optional)

Preparation

Experiment with markers in your classroom to find some that write well on balloons. Blow up as many balloons as there are students in your class plus a few extras. Poke the end of a pipe cleaner through the lip of each balloon. Use these "stems" to help turn the balloons into a "bouquet." Put the balloons in a vase or tie them to the back of a chair.

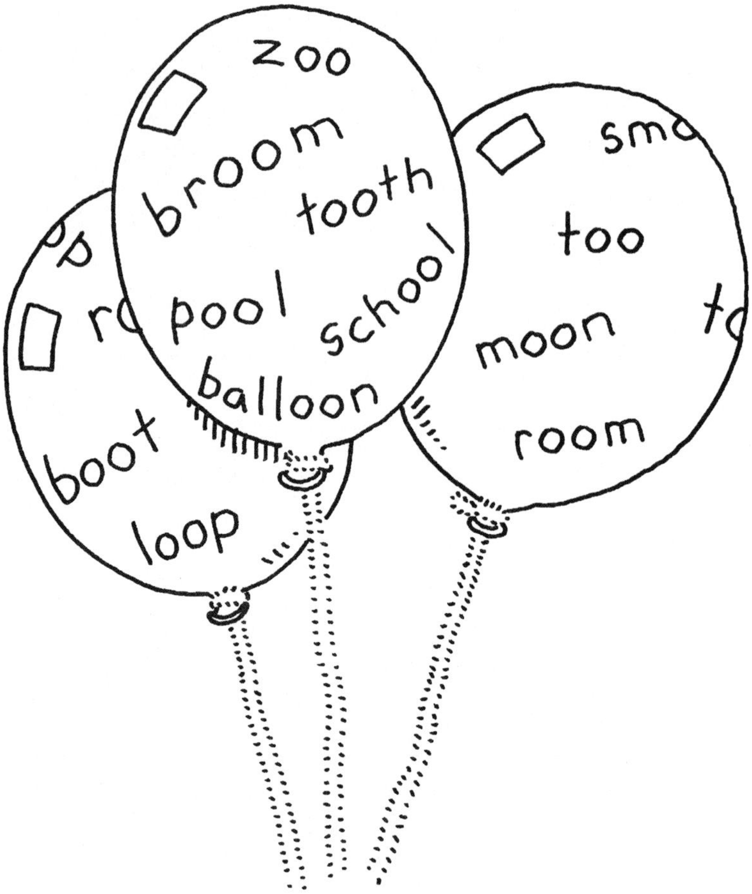

Have students brainstorm /oo/ words (as in *balloon*), and write their suggestions on the board. Give each student a balloon, and invite students to use a marker to write five to ten *oo* words on their balloon. Take the class outside, and have students read their *oo* words to a partner. Then, invite students to pop their balloon by sitting on it. Boom!

Oo words include the following:

balloon	fool	moon	root	tool
boom	goose	moose	school	toot
boot	hoop	noon	smooth	tooth
broom	hoot	pool	soon	zoo
cool	loop	roof	stool	zoom
food	loose	room	too	

Look, a Book Crook!

oo Vowel Digraph

Have students brainstorm words that have the /oo/ sound, as in *book, look,* and *foot,* and write their suggestions on the board. Have each student write on a piece of paper *Look, a crook took my good book!* and then choose a favorite classroom book. Have students take their book to their seat, add the title to their paper, and then return the book to its place. Give each student a large brown grocery sack. Have students place their paper in their sack. Have students put all the sacks in a common location at the front of the class or by your desk. Have them put their head down and close their eyes. Quietly take one student's paper, read it, hide it in your desk, and then have students open their eyes. Give clues to the identity of the book by naming the author, describing a character, or reading a sentence from the book. If a student recognizes the book as the one he or she chose, he or she can be the next "crook." If not, offer further clues. When the book is identified, return the paper to the student's bag, and continue until most students have had an opportunity to be the crook.

Oo words include the following:

book	crook	hood	shook	wood
brook	foot	hook	stood	wool
cook	good	look	took	

Have the student lay out several books. Have him or her write Look, a crook took my good book! *on a piece of paper. While the student closes his or her eyes, take one book away. Have the student read the paper and take two guesses to figure out which book is missing. Give clues to describe the book if the student does not name the book in two guesses. Mix the books up and play again.*

Materials

- ✔ paper
- ✔ storybooks
- ✔ large brown grocery sacks

Preparation

none

Know Flakes

ow Vowel Digraph

Materials

- ✔ white butcher paper or plain chart paper
- ✔ scissors
- ✔ sentence strip (optional)
- ✔ white paper

Preparation

Use the directions for the small snowflakes to make a large snowflake from a piece of white butcher paper or plain chart paper. Write several *ow* words on one side of the snowflake. Display the snowflake on the chalkboard or a bulletin board.

Write *snowflake* on the board or on a sentence strip. Underline or highlight the *ow* in *snowflake*. Tell students the *ow* makes the long *o* sound. Read aloud the *ow* words on the snowflake, and have volunteers underline the *ow* in each word. Then, give each student a piece of white paper, and have students use the following directions to make their own snowflake:

1. Cut the paper to an 8½" (21.5 cm) square.
2. Fold one corner to the opposite corner to create a large triangle.
3. Fold the triangle in half to make a smaller triangle.

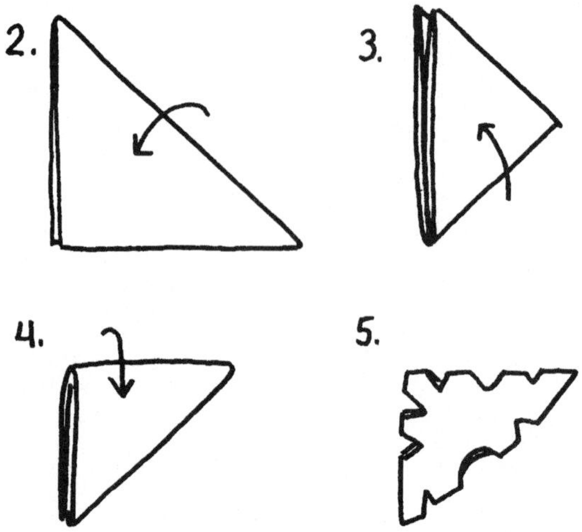

4. Fold the triangle in half again to make a smaller triangle.

5. Cut out small shapes of your choice anywhere on the triangle except the tips.

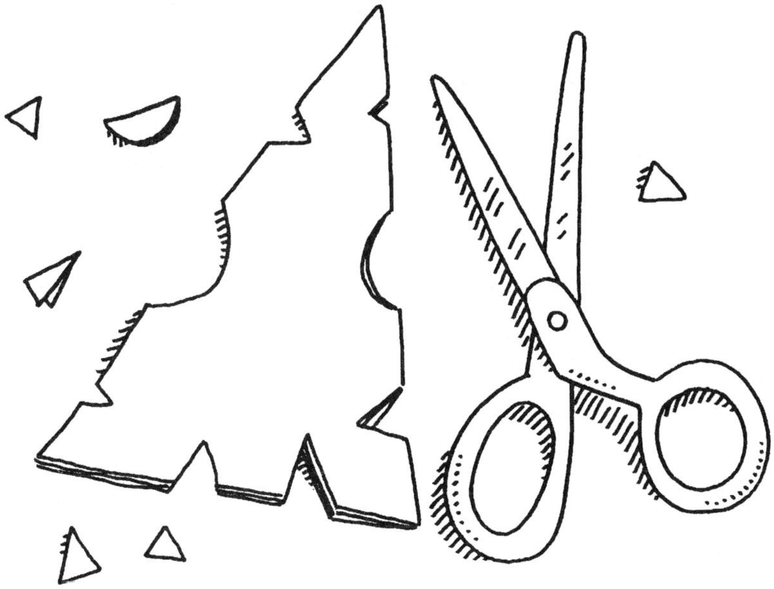

6. Unfold your snowflake.

Have students write *ow* words anywhere on their completed snowflake. Display the "Know Flakes" throughout the classroom.

Ow words include the following:

blow	flow	know	own	snow
bow	glow	low	row	throw
bowl	grow	mow	show	
crow	grown	owe	slow	

Have the student paint over the words with glow-in-the-dark paint (available at fabric or craft stores) to create a "Glow Know Flake."

Our Wow Cow

ou/ow Vowel Digraphs

Materials

- ✔ Our Wow Cow reproducible (page 51)
- ✔ overhead transparency and projector
- ✔ marker
- ✔ butcher paper
- ✔ clear tape
- ✔ large index cards
- ✔ light-colored construction paper
- ✔ scissors
- ✔ glue

Preparation

Photocopy the Our Wow Cow reproducible onto an overhead transparency. Project the image onto a large piece of butcher paper and trace it with a marker. Then, flip the transparency over and trace the image again to create two cows facing each other. Write across the top of the butcher paper *Our Wow Cows!* Tape a large index card beneath each cow. Label one card *ou* and the other *ow*.

Write several *ow* and *ou* words on the board. Read these to students, and ask them what vowel sound they have in common. Underline the *ow* and *ou* in the words. Then, have students brainstorm additional *ow* and *ou* words, and add their suggestions to the list. Give each student a piece of light-colored construction paper, and invite students to cut out "spots" in a variety of shapes. Have students write an *ou* or *ow* word on each spot, and invite them to tape or glue the spots to the corresponding cow. You'll have a "mooo-st" unusual addition to your classroom.

Ou/ow words include the following:

about	down	growl	ouch	scout
bow	flour	hour	out	shout
brown	flower	how	ow	shower
cloud	found	howl	owl	sound
clown	frown	loud	pound	sprout
cow	gown	mouth	proud	towel
crown	ground	now	round	town

Our Wow Cow

Mr. Y, the Mystery Guy

y Sounds

Materials

- ✔ Mr. Y, the Mystery Guy reproducible (page 53)
- ✔ overhead transparency and projector
- ✔ chart paper
- ✔ sunglasses
- ✔ pointer

Preparation

Photocopy the Mr. Y, the Mystery Guy reproducible onto an overhead transparency. Divide a piece of chart paper into three columns. In the first column write *yard, yes,* and *yellow.* In the middle column write *by, cry,* and *fly.* In the last column write *Sally, silly,* and *sunny.*

Display the chart paper, and read the three columns aloud with students. Invite students to tell you what sound the *y* makes in each column. Have students brainstorm additional words to add to each column. Discuss which of their suggestions belong in which column and why. Display the Mr. Y, the Mystery Guy transparency, and teach students the refrain to the rap song on the reproducible. Invite a volunteer to wear sunglasses and use a pointer to highlight the *y* words as the class chants the song. Encourage students to clap a beat as they chant.

Y words include the following:

yarn	you	dry	why	penny
yawn	yuck	my	giggly	pretty
yet	by	try	happy	sunny

Mr. Y, the Mystery Guy

When you start a word like *yard, yes,* or *yellow,*

You make the */y/* sound, little fellow.

Refrain:
Y, oh Y, you are a tricky little guy.
You can sound like */y/*, or *e*, or *i*.

When a word is little, like *fly, by,* or *cry,*

You make your *i* sound, my sly guy.

Refrain

When a word is longer, like *Sally, silly,* or *sunny,*

You make your *e* sound. You're so funny.

Refrain

Castle Door

Silent *t*

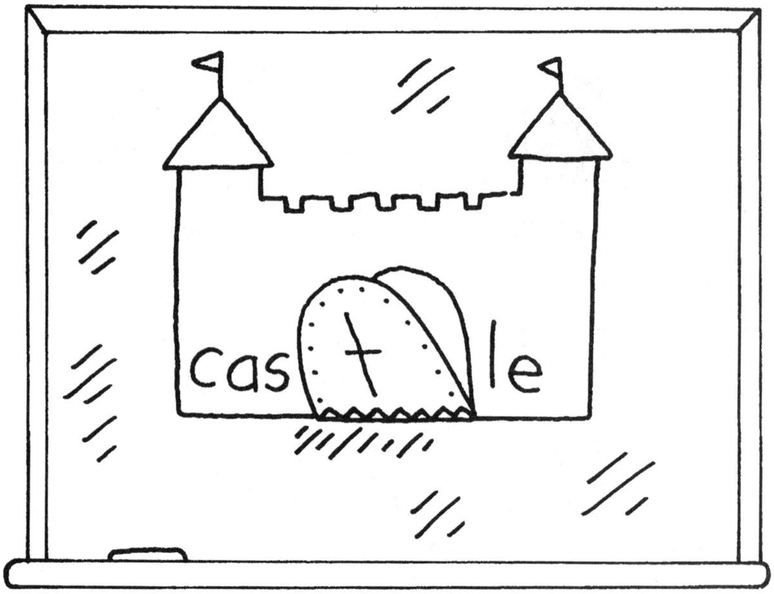

Materials

- ✔ file folder
- ✔ scissors
- ✔ markers
- ✔ chart paper
- ✔ clear tape

Preparation

Hold a file folder horizontally, and draw an arch that begins and ends at the folder's spine. Cut out the arch, cutting through both sides of the folder. Write a large lowercase *t* on the front of the arch, and use markers to decorate it to look like a drawbridge. Write silent *t* words on chart paper.

Display the chart paper, and read aloud the first word to students. Then, tell students you are going to sound out the word slowly. Invite them to tell you which letter is not making its sound in this word. Read aloud the first word again, slowly emphasizing each sound heard in the word. Ask volunteers to tell you which letter is silent. Read aloud the next word, and invite students to listen for the /t/ sound. Ask students to raise their hands if they hear it. Tell students that a few letters are silent when they are in a particular place in a word and *t* is usually silent when it comes before *ch* or *le*. Read aloud the rest of the list. Then, draw on the chalkboard the outline of a simple castle. Tape the back flap of the drawbridge door to the chalkboard in the center of the castle. Have students take turns writing a silent *t* word in the castle with the *t* on the door serving as the silent *t* in the word they write. Invite the class to read each word. Then, open the door and have the class say the word without the *t*. Invite students to discuss whether or not the words sound the same with and without the *t*.

Silent *t* words include the following:

batch	catch	latch	patch
bristle	fasten	listen	rustle
bustle	glisten	match	watch
castle	itch	often	whistle

Chalk Walk

Silent *l*

Write silent *l* words on the board, grouping the words by rime families (e.g., *alf, alm, alk,* and *olk*), and read aloud the list to students. Invite volunteers to locate and underline the rimes the words have in common. Tell students that the *l* is silent in these words. Give each student three to four index cards, and have students write a silent *l* word on each card. Collect the cards, divide the class into teams of four or five, and take students to the playground. Give each team a piece of chalk, and assign them an area. Invite them to draw a curved path. Place index cards along each team's path. Have students take turns going on a "Chalk Walk" by having them follow their path, pick up each card, and read it. After each student finishes the walk, have him or her replace the cards for the next student.

Silent *l* words include the following:

calf	calm	chalk	folk
half	palm	stalk	yolk
		talk	
		walk	

Materials

✔ index cards

✔ chalk

Preparation

Present this activity on a day that's not too windy. Read through the silent *l* words. Some of these words may be acceptably pronounced with or without the *l*.

Soft like a Lamb

Silent *b*

Materials

- ✔ permanent marker
- ✔ 16 brightly colored, large plastic cups
- ✔ cotton balls
- ✔ pebbles

Preparation

Use a permanent marker to write the following letters on separate cups: *a, b, c, d, e, h, i, l, m, n, o, p, r, t.* Write *u* on each of the two remaining cups.

Line up the four cups that spell *lamb*. Place cotton balls in the bottom of the *b* cup. Pass around additional cotton balls, and have each student feel how soft they are. Relate the softness of the cotton to that of a lamb's wool. Have a student drop one pebble in each of the cups. Students will hear a noise in each, until they get to the *b* cup which will be silent. Explain that just as the pebble is silent in the *b* cup, so is *b* silent in *lamb*. Invite volunteers to arrange the cups to spell the other silent *b* words listed below. Have students take turns dropping pebbles into the cups, blending the sounds as they go, and reading the silent *b* word before passing the pebbles to the next student.

Silent *b* words include the following:

climb	crumb	lamb	numb	thumb
comb	doubt	limb	plumber	

Wrestling with *W*s

Silent *w*

Materials

- ✔ white watercolor or tempera paint
- ✔ small cups
- ✔ lined paper
- ✔ cotton swabs

Preparation

Pour a small amount of white paint into a small cup for each group.

Write a list of silent *w* words on the board, leaving out the *w*s. Say the words. Have volunteers add *w*s to the words on the board. Reread the words, and invite students to consider whether the words sound different. Divide the class into small groups of three or four students. Give students lined paper, and have them copy ten words off the board. Distribute a cotton swab to each student and a small cup of white paint to each group. Have students use their cotton swab to dab white paint on each silent *w*. Tell students that the pencil *w* will be visible through the paint, but the paint will help them remember not to pronounce it.

Silent *w* words include the following:

answer	wreath	wrench	wrinkle	written
sword	wreck	wrestle	wrist	wrong
wrap	wren	wring	write	wrote

Knee Discovery

Silent *k*

Materials

- ✔ chart paper
- ✔ adhesive bandages
- ✔ lined paper
- ✔ scissors (optional)

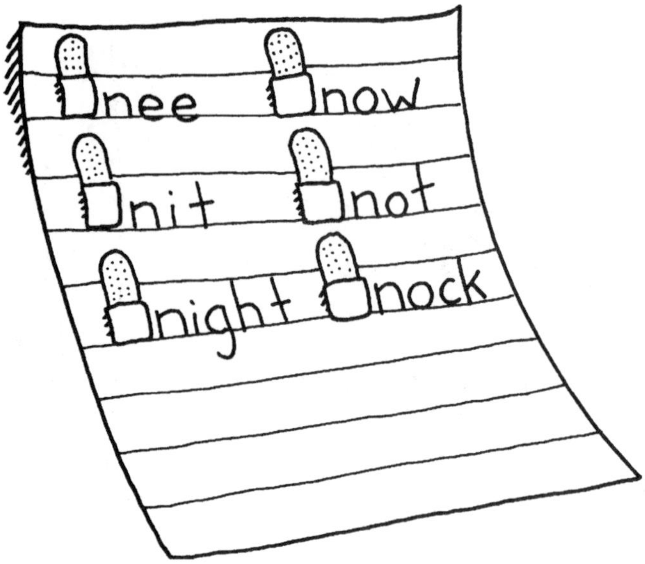

Preparation

Draw on chart paper a picture of a bent knee with an adhesive bandage and a long leg. Write silent *k* words in a column down the leg.

Display the chart paper, and have students read the silent *k* words with you. Then, give volunteers adhesive bandages to put over the silent *k*s on the leg. Invite students to discuss whether or not the words sound different without the *k*. Give each student a piece of lined paper and five or six adhesive bandages, and have students write several of the silent *k* words on their paper. Invite students to cover each silent *k* with an adhesive bandage. Show students how to attach the top of the adhesive bandage only, letting the rest of it hang over the *k* so students can peek at the missing *k*. They can bend the second half of the adhesive strip under the bandage, or trim it off with scissors.

Silent *k* words include the following:

knapsack	knew	knit	knock	knowledge
knee	knife	knives	knot	known
kneel	knight	knob	know	knuckles

Gnaw It

Silent *g*

Write a list of silent *g* words on the board, and read the words aloud. Have volunteers identify the silent letter. Give each student a piece of lined paper and a licorice string. Have students write silent *g* words on their paper without the *g*s. Encourage students to use their licorice to form the *g*s on their paper, pressing the licorice onto the paper. Have each student read aloud his or her silent *g* words and gnaw on the rest of the licorice while other students read.

Silent *g* words include the following:

align	gnarled	gnat	resign
design	gnash	gnaw	sign

Materials

- ✔ lined paper
- ✔ three to four bags of long licorice strings

Preparation

none

Mini-Book Assembly

Photocopy and trim the mini-books (pages 62–67). Have students follow these steps to make each mini-book:

1. Fold the paper in half.
2. Cut along the dotted line halfway through the folded paper.
3. Hold the paper with the cut at the top. Fold the left flap forward and the right flap backward.
4. Keeping the flaps folded, open the paper so you can see the blank side.
5. Fold the paper in half so the pictures face outward.
6. Fold the paper in half again. Be sure page one is in front.

1

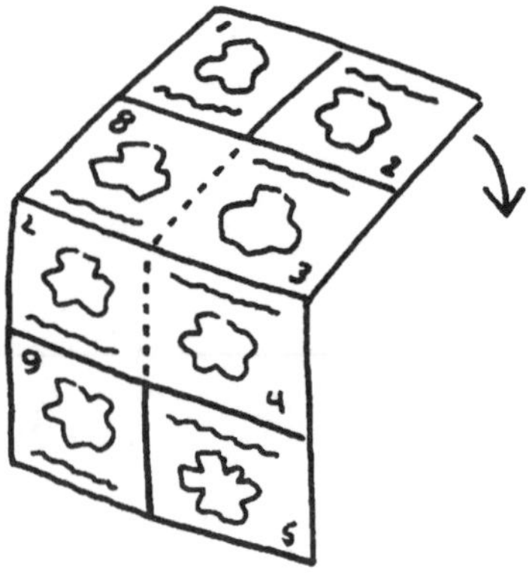

2

3

4

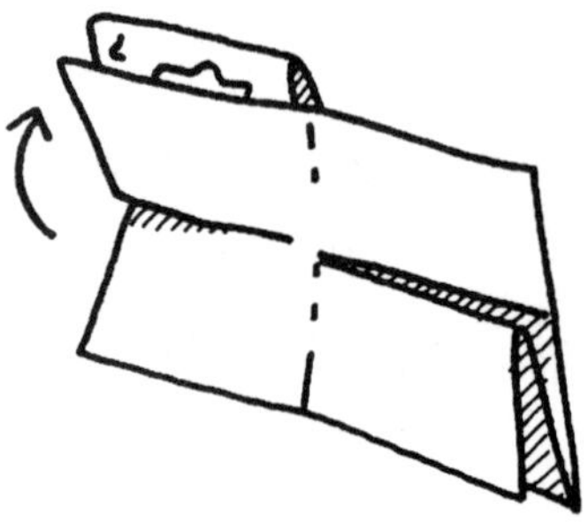

5

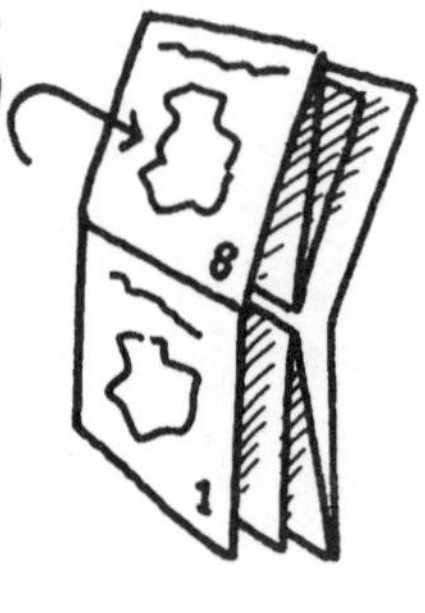

6

Mini-Book Activity Ideas

Enjoy these mini-book activities with your students:

- Photocopy a class set of the mini-book, and distribute one to each student. Model how to assemble the book, and invite students to do so. Read the mini-book with students, and then invite them to underline or highlight a specific digraph or blend.

- Photocopy and cut into individual pages enough copies of the book to give a page to each student. As you read each page, have students identify the repeating digraph or blend. For each of the digraphs or blends repeated in the book, ask those students who have that digraph or blend in many of the words on their page to underline or highlight it. After all students have located their repeating digraph or blend, give each student an index card on which to copy the words that begin with that digraph or blend. Tape four large squares of shelf paper, sticky side out, onto a wall. Stick a letter card representing each digraph or blend to the top of each shelf-paper square. Ask students to stick their index card to the square that has their digraph or blend on it.

- Photocopy the mini-book to an overhead transparency, and cut it into individual frames. Display two pages at a time, matching the repeated digraphs or blends. Have students sit in a circle, and have a large ball of yarn ready. Read aloud the first two pages, and invite students to identify the repeated digraphs or blends. Then, challenge them to think of other words that have the same digraphs or blends. Have each student share his or her contribution. As students are sharing, roll the ball of yarn over to them. As more words are generated, the "web" of yarn grows. Continue until all digraphs or blends in the mini-book are reviewed, and take a photo of the completed web.

Mini-Book One

ch

5

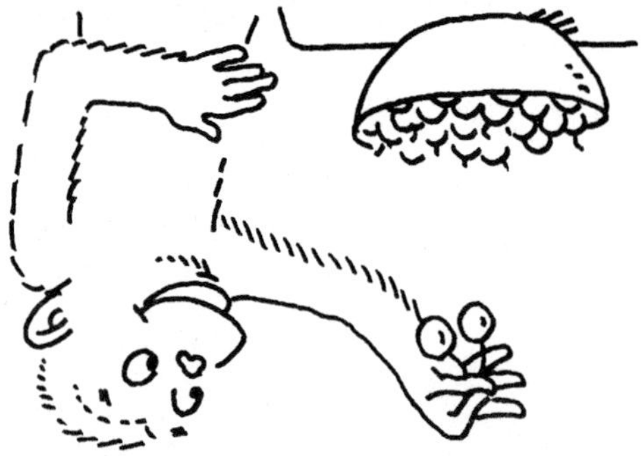

Chip chooses cherries

and cheese to munch.

6

4

Chip the chimp stomps.

Chip is cheerful

7

3

Chip the chimp scatters.

when he chews his lunch.

8

2

Chip the chimp chomps.

Chip the chimp chatters.

1

Mini-Book Two

sh

I wish I were a fish.

1

A fish who loves to wish.

2

A fish who loves to splash.

3

A fish who loves to thrash.

4

A fish who shines

5

so shimmering and fine.

6

I wish I were a shiny, splashy,

7

swishy, wishy fish.

8

Mini-Book Three

dr

5

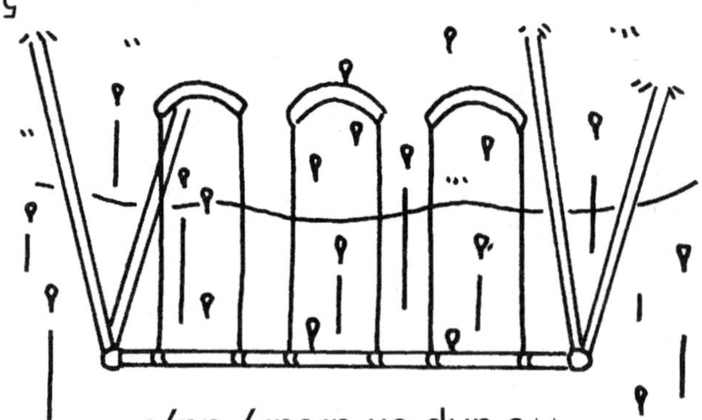

We drip on dreary days

so the children cannot play.

6

4

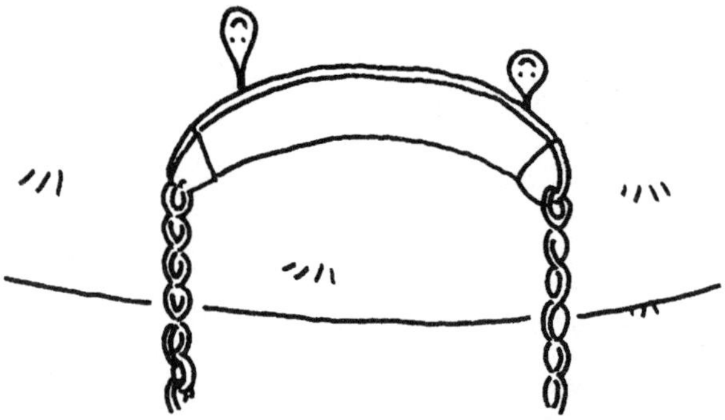

I drop and I dribble.

Drippy Drop, dropping Drip

7

3

I drip and I drizzle.

drizzling down the drain.

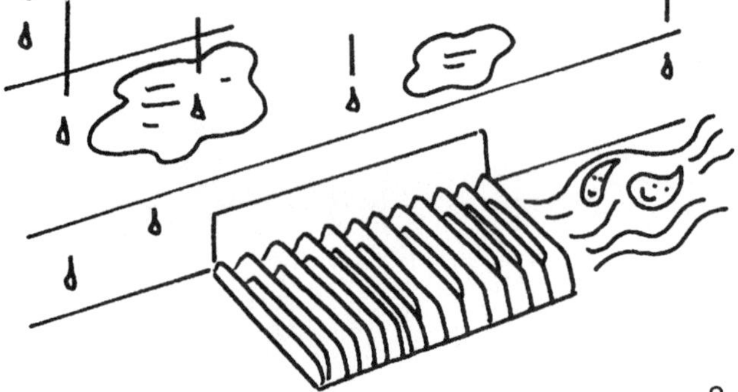

8

2

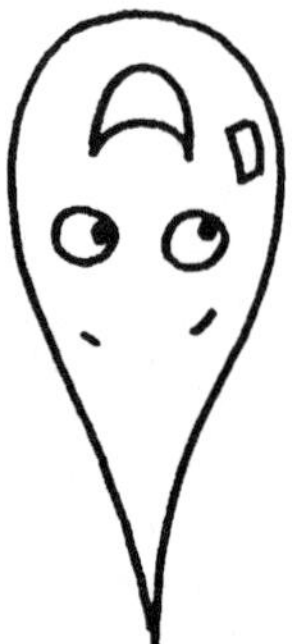

I am Drop.

I am Drip.

1

Mini-Book Four

gr, sl, cr, cl, br, st, bl

A green vine grew.

1

It slipped and slid

2

across a crooked creek.

3

It climbed a cliff

4

and broke its branches.

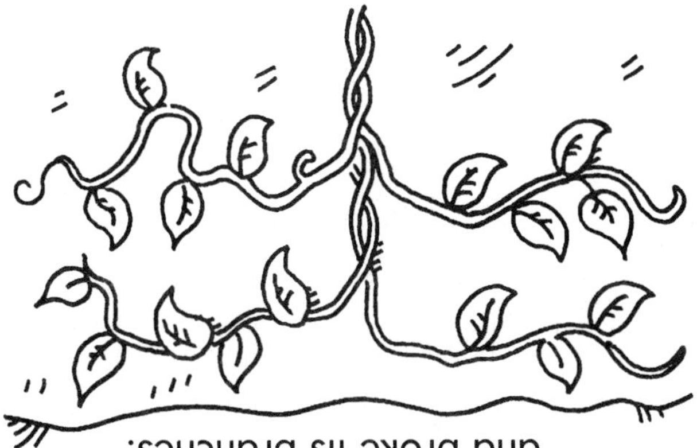

5

It stood still and started

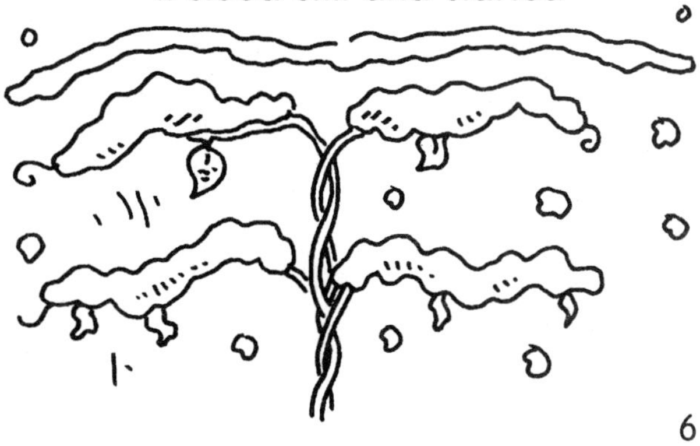

6

to blossom and bloom.

7

It grows great grapes.

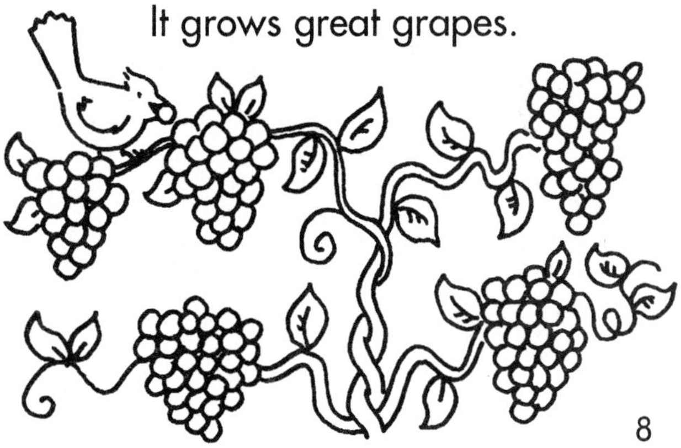

8

Mini-Book Five

bl, cl, cr, dr, fl, sk, silent k, silent l

The dragon blows flames

1

in the dreary, cloudy sky.

2

He flies in loops

3

way up high.

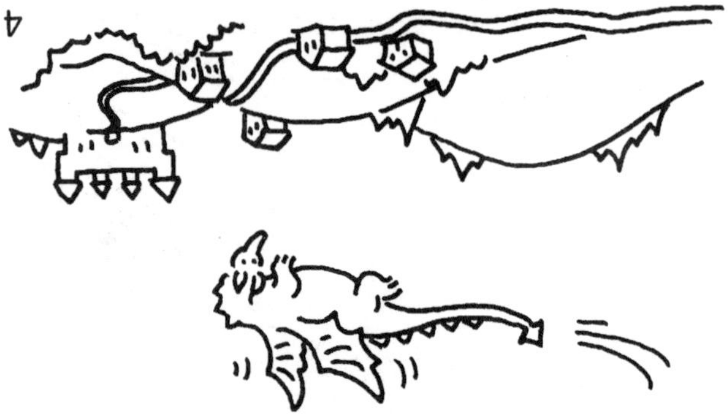

4

He hears the knight walking,

5

clink, clank, crunch.

6

They do not clash or fight.

7

They meet for lunch.

8

Mini-Book Six

tr, cl, pl, sp, st

5

It stopped and stayed

at places to play.

6

4

and sparkling spaces.

Then with a clack

7

3

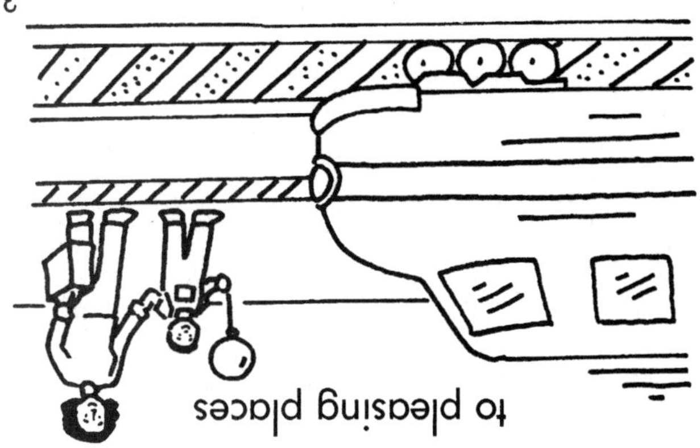

to pleasing places

it got back on track.

8

2

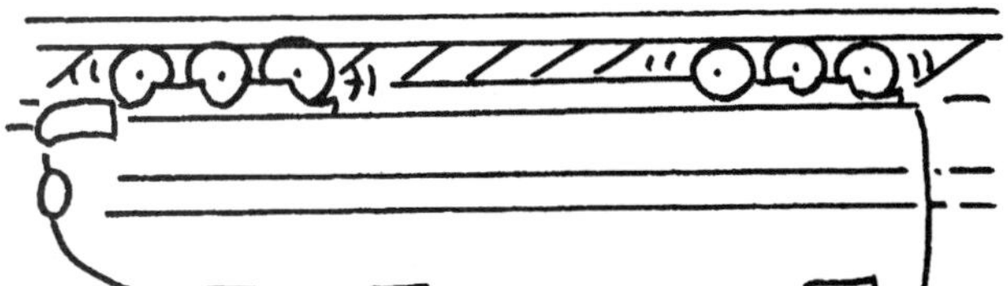

with clicks and clacks

The train traveled on tracks

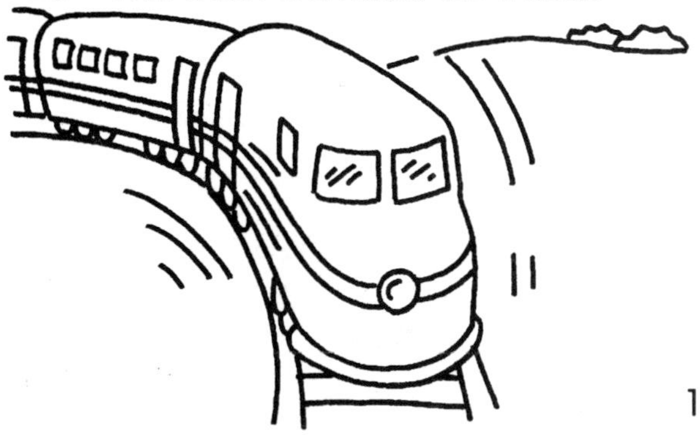

1

Picture- and Letter-Card Activities

Here are a few activities to get students started with the picture and letter cards (pages 71–80). Additional cards can be created by gluing pictures from magazines or catalogs to index cards. Laminate the cards or cover them with clear shelf paper for greater durability.

- Index Box—Obtain several index-card boxes that include alphabet tabs. Write additional phonemes, such as vowel digraphs and blends, on blank tabs. Attach a small envelope to the back of each box. Photocopy picture cards to paper or card stock, and cut them apart. Make one set of cards for each box. Place the picture cards into the envelope. Have students take the picture cards from the envelope and file each one behind the corresponding letter tab.

- Memory—Photocopy and cut apart the picture and letter cards for the phonemes or blends on which you want students to focus. Divide the class into small groups. Invite a student to shuffle the cards and lay them facedown on the table. Have students take turns picking up pairs and trying to match phonemes or blends. Cards that do not match are placed facedown again. The player with the most pairs at the end of the game gets to shuffle the cards and lay them down again to start a new game.

- Go Fish—Photocopy and cut apart the picture and letter cards for the phonemes or blends on which you want students to focus. Consider adding additional picture cards. Make a set for each small group of two to four students. Divide the class into groups of two to four students, and give each group a set of cards. Tell students the object of the game is to make pairs and be the first to run out of cards. Have one student in each group shuffle the cards and deal five cards to each player. Invite students to try to form pairs from the cards in their hand and place pairs on the table. Invite the first student in each group to look at his or her hand and choose a card to try to match. For example, a student with the *shark* card asks another student in the group *Do you have any /sh/ cards in your hand?* If he or she has the card, it is given to the student asking for it. If not, the player asking has to *go fish* by drawing the top card off the remaining pile. Play continues until all of the cards have been matched.

- Flashing Phonemes—Photocopy, cut apart, and distribute to each student the letter cards for the phonemes or blends you want students to review. Photocopy the corresponding picture cards on overhead transparencies. Cut the transparencies into individual picture cards for your own use. Have students lay the letter cards faceup on their desk. Display a picture card on an overhead projector, say the name of the picture aloud, and ask students to hold up the matching letter card for the phoneme or blend heard at the beginning of the word. This can also be done for the middle or end of the word.

- Folder Sorts—Write on the tab of a folder phonemes or blends for students to review, and open the folder lengthwise. Glue matching letter cards across the top of the folder, one picture card under each letter card, and an envelope on the outside of the folder. Cut out the remaining picture cards, and store them in the envelope. Invite students to take the picture cards from the envelope and sort them in the appropriate column. Have students show you their work when they are done, and discuss with them the choices they made.

- Phoneme Mobile—Photocopy the picture cards for the phonemes or blends you want students to review. Distribute a hanger, string or yarn, picture cards, and the corresponding letter cards to each student. Invite students to match each picture card to the appropriate letter card, color the cards, punch a hole in the top and bottom of each card, and string each phoneme or blend group along one piece of string or yarn. Finally, have students tie the strings to their hanger and decorate it with more string or yarn.

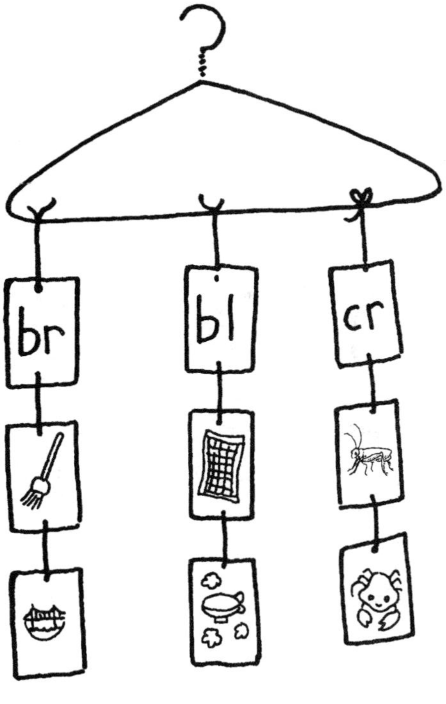

- Room Search—Photocopy and cut apart picture cards for the phonemes or blends on which you want students to focus. Hide them around the room, and invite students to try to find matching pairs. Have students who found cards for the same sound, such as the *ch* cards, gather in one spot or be in a cooperative group for that day.

- Mystery Necklace—Photocopy and cut apart the picture cards for all the phonemes or blends. Punch holes in the top and bottom center of each one, and string together the cards with the same phonemes or blends on a yard (meter) length of yarn to make a "necklace." Place a necklace on each student so that the cards are worn on his or her back. Then, invite students to circulate, read each other's cards, and give each other clues to help guess what phoneme or blend they have. Suggest that students offer other words that contain the same phoneme or blend to give clues without telling the actual picture on the card.
- Flash Cards—Photocopy and cut apart the picture cards for several phonemes or blends. Write the phoneme or blend represented by each picture on the back of each card, and invite students to use the cards as flash cards. Have students look at each picture card, say the name of the picture, decide which phoneme or blend is heard in that word, and check the back for accuracy.
- Phonemic Map—Write the phonemes or blends you want students to review on the inside of index cards folded in half. Attach a sign sticker, such as *stop* or *yield,* to each card. Divide the class into small groups, and have each group draw cars on index cards and make a big map on chart or butcher paper that includes streets, parks, and other items of their choice. Give each small group a set of index-card "signs" to place along the streets. Ask students to drive their "car" around their map. Ask students to stop at each sign, open the card, read the phoneme or blend, and say words that have that sound in it. For example, a student might read *ang* and say *clang* and *sang.*

Picture Cards: *th*

th

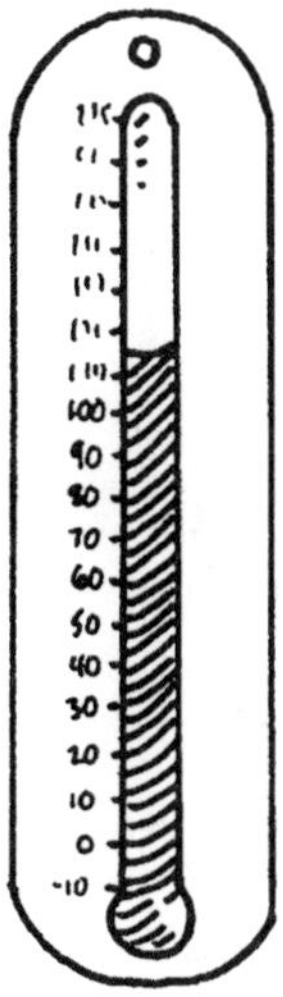

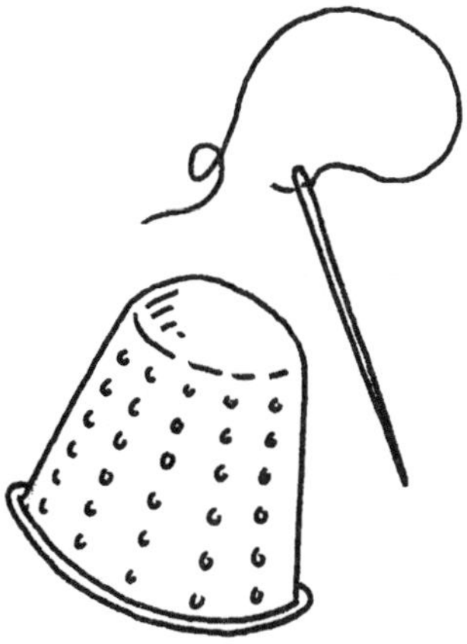

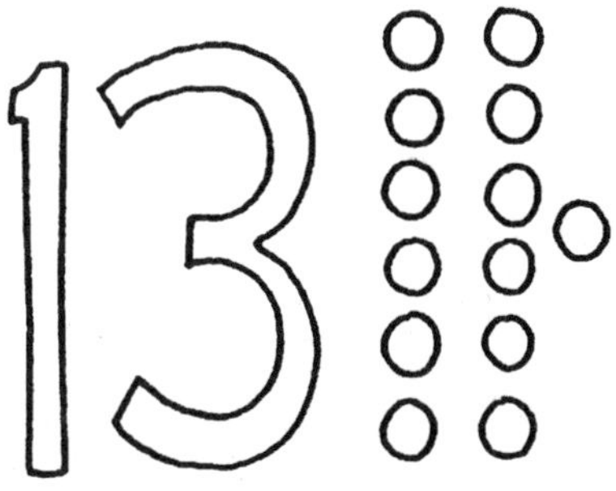

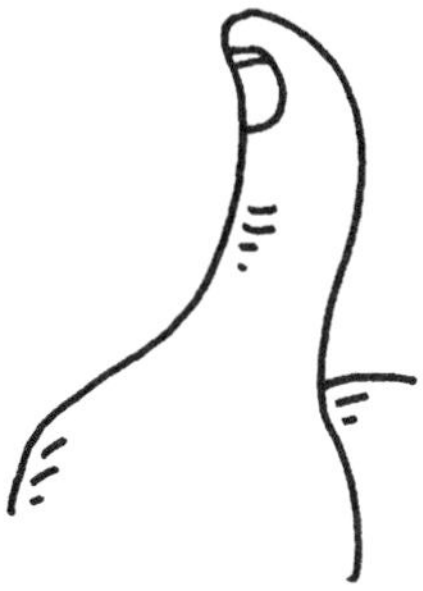

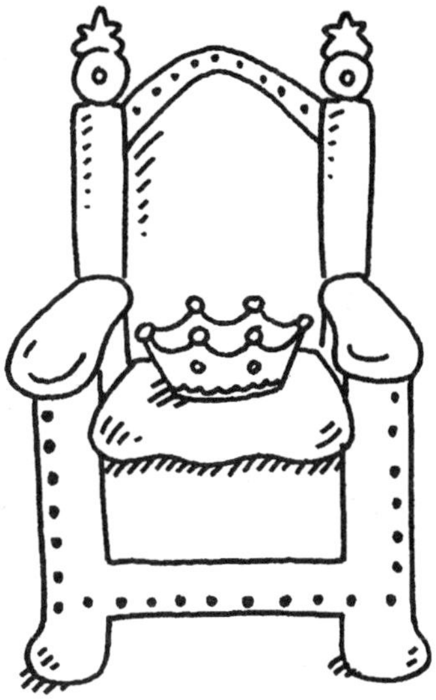

Picture Cards: *ch*

ch		
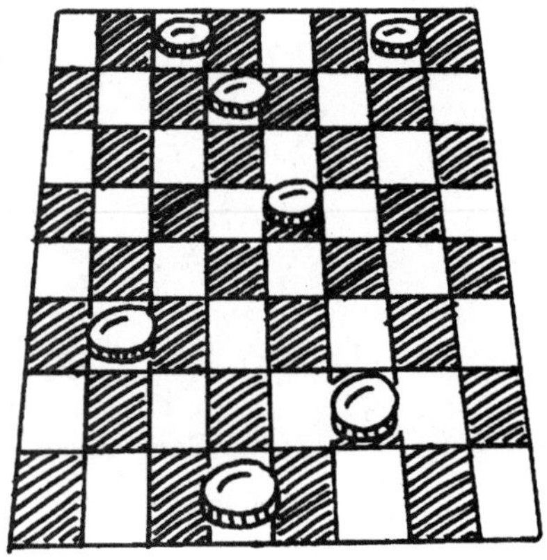		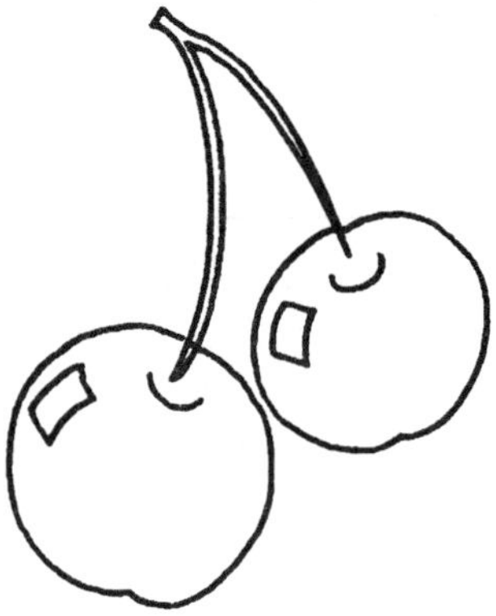
	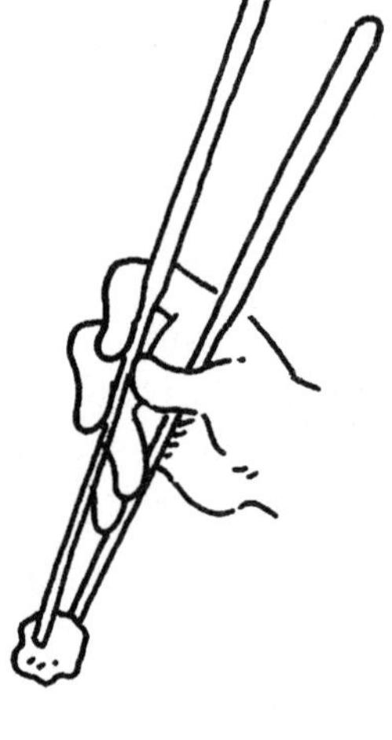	

Picture Cards: *sh, wh*

sh		
	wh	

Picture Cards: *ng, ph, sn, sp*

ng	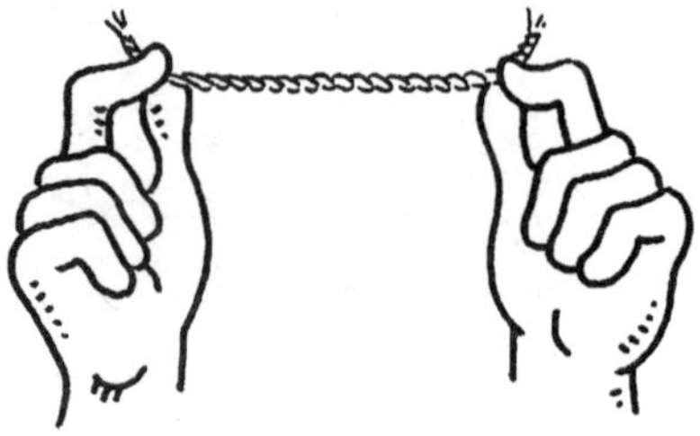	
ph		sn
	sp	

Picture Cards: *bl, br*

bl

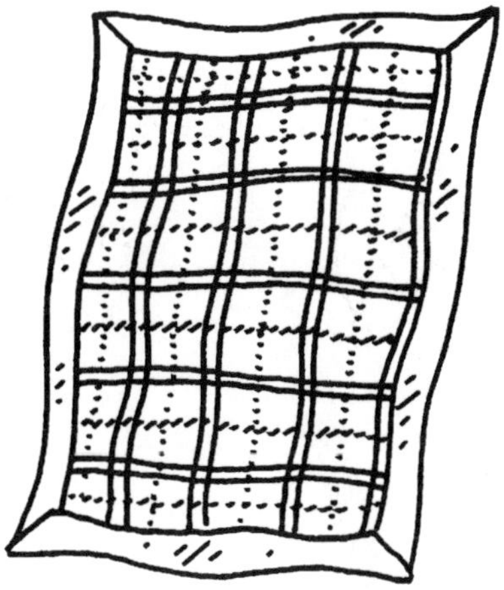

br

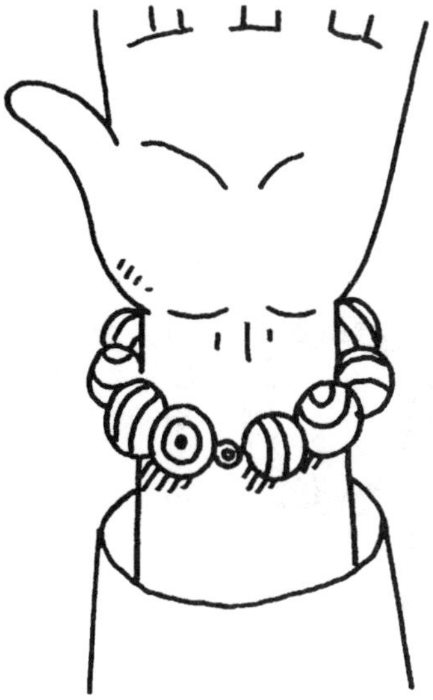

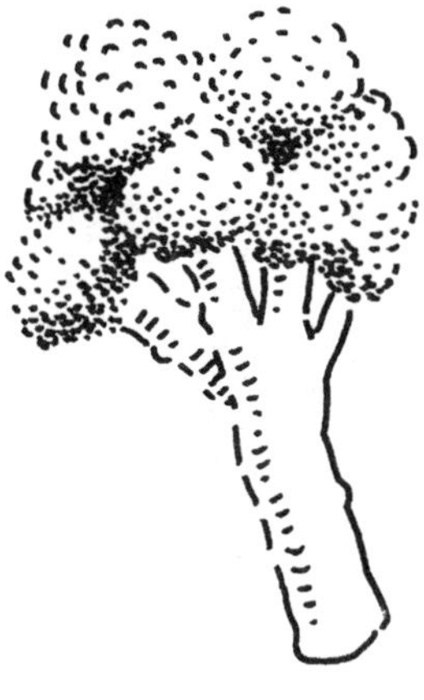

Picture Cards: *cl, cr*

cl

cr

Picture Cards: *dr, fl*

dr

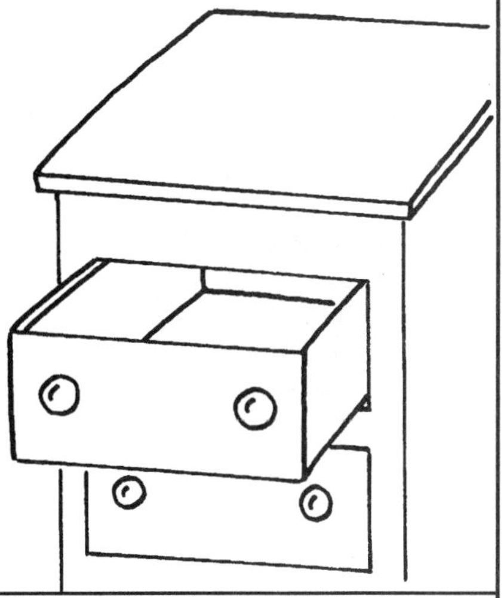

fl

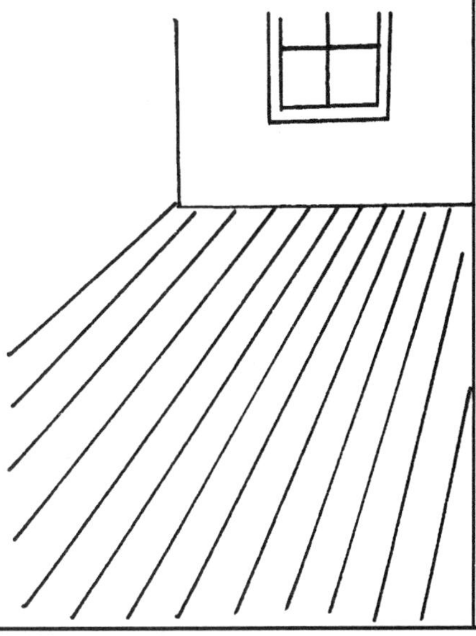

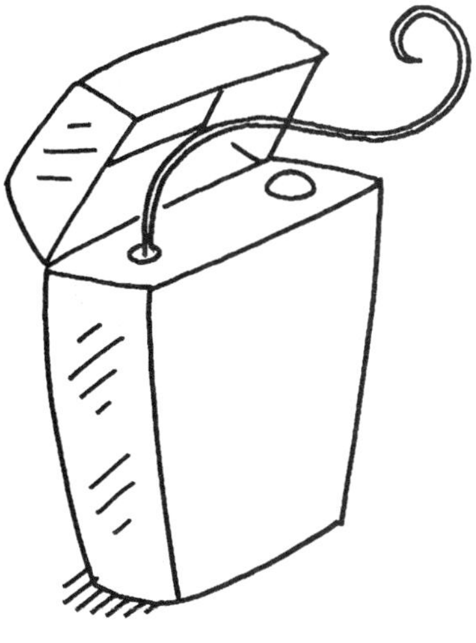

Picture Cards: *sk, sl, gr*

sk

sl

gr

Picture Cards: *fr, tr*

fr		
tr		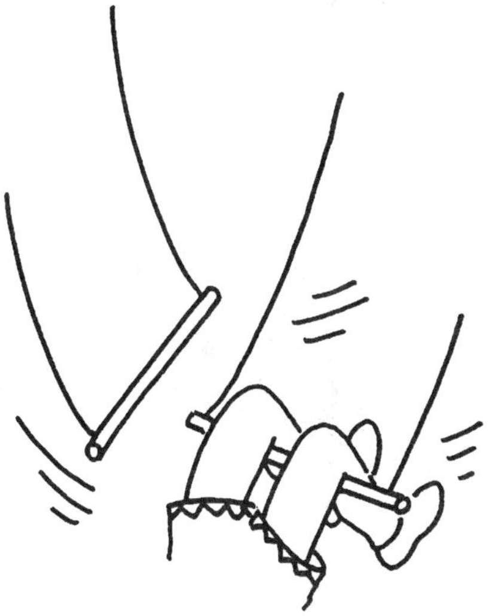
		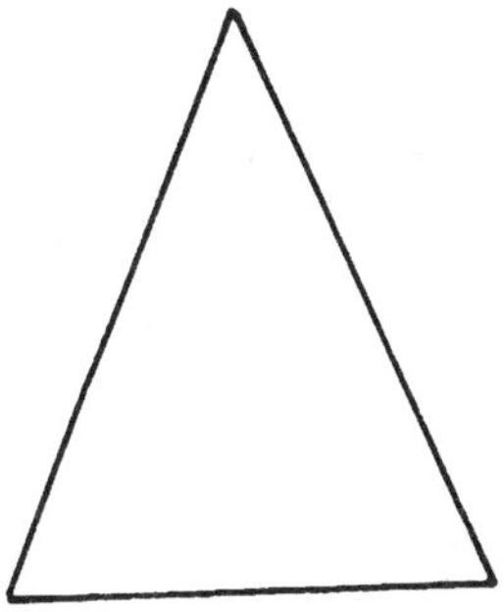

Picture Cards: *st, pr*

st

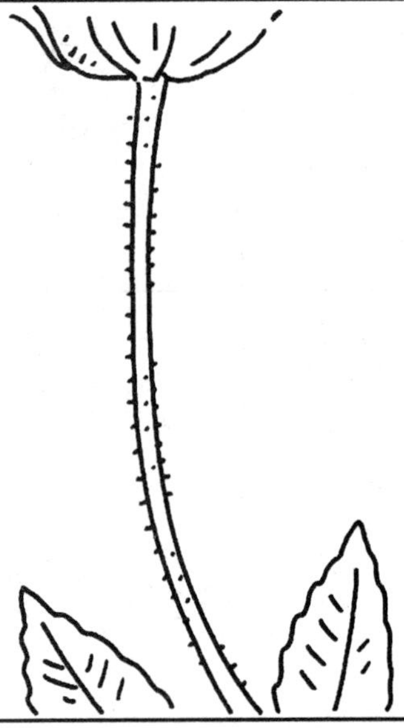

pr

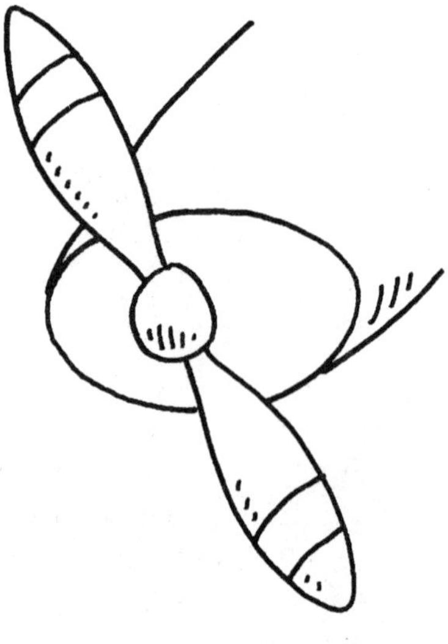